A
Shriek
in the
Forest
Night

Wilderness
Encounters

R. D. Lawrence

Published in 1996 by
Stoddart Publishing Co. Limited
34 Lesmill Road
Toronto, Canada
M3B 2T6
Tel. (416) 445-3333
Fax (416) 445-5967

Canadian Cataloguing in Publication Data

Lawrence, R.D. (Ronald Douglas), 1921–
A shriek in the forest night: wilderness encounters

ISBN 0-7737-2941-0

1. Zoology – Canada.   2. Lawrence, R.D. (Ronald Douglas), 1921–
I. Title.

QL791.L3 1996   591.971   C96-930167-7

Cover Design: the boy 100 &
Tannice Goddard
Computer Graphics: Mary Bowness
Illustrations: Tannice Goddard

Printed and bound in United States of America

*Stoddart Publishing gratefully acknowledges the support of the Canada
Council, the Ontario Ministry of Citizenship, Culture and Recreation,
Ontario Arts Council, and Ontario Publishing Centre in the development
of writing and publishing in Canada.*

For my wife, Sharon, who supplies the love
and the tender touch that means so much
to every wildling that comes to us

Contents

Prologue

In the late summer of 1975, after I had been desk-bound while completing a book, I decided to spend some time in the boreal forests of northern British Columbia near the Spatsizi Plateau. I would do some field work there while relaxing in the wilderness.

Entering the gloom of the forestal understory, I cleared a small space for my tent and settled down to study a world that I had previously only passed through as a traveler. Of course, I couldn't explore the entire vast region, but instead confined myself to an area that boasted tall trees, rocky crags, a luscious understory, and, near my pitched tent, a crystal-clear lake that was about half a mile long by a quarter of a mile wide. In a place that contained hundreds of lakes, *my* waterway, as I soon began to think of it, was unnamed and not found on my topographic map.

One hot afternoon, about a week after I had been there, I decided to dive into the lake, intending only to cool myself off. But as I reached the sandy bottom I became fascinated by a number of small organisms that moved about undisturbed by my arrival. The first was a crayfish, a brownish, lobster-like creature that was about five inches long. As I went closer, it dived smoothly into a hole that it had drilled neatly in the sandy bottom. Next, a colorful sunfish some four inches long passed near me swiftly and elegantly as it aimed itself upward. The fish reached the surface in seconds and, mouth agape, snatched an insect that was dimpling the surface with its thin seemingly ungainly legs. Although indistinct, I knew it was a water strider.

As I swam slowly along the bottom, I spotted a sluggish, long-bodied creature that probably measured one-and-a-half inches. It was the larva of a crane fly. Seconds later, a leech came into view and began undulating toward me, evidently attracted by the chemical scents (pheromones) that humans and all other mammals, birds, and insects produce constantly. I did not relish playing host to a leech, and at that moment my lungs reminded me that I needed air, but I might have waited until the rather elegant creature sought to sip my blood.

Kicking off from the bottom, I shot upward, leaving the bloodsucker well behind. When my head broke the surface I found myself almost eye to eye with a startled painted turtle, a beautiful animal that is usually sluggish on land or walking along a floating log, but swift as a fish when startled. One second we were looking at each from a distance of about ten inches, the next my neighbour dove and was immediately invisible.

On shore, I toweled myself to rub some warmth into my body, for the lake water was cold. I was reminded of the time when I had been diving in the Red Sea off the reef of Sharm el Sheikh, which is located off the southernmost point of Egypt's Sinai Peninsula. I had gone there to study sharks, but each time I dived I became captivated by the fascinating variety of life forms that surrounded me, the majority of which I had never seen before.

I sat on a log and watched the surface of the shimmering lake, seeing again in my mind's eye the life of the Red Sea — the flotillas of multicoloured fish feeding on marine plants much as the deer that now lived near me and grazed on abundant grasses and leaves. I recalled that I had watched on many occasions while other fish dined on polyps after crushing coral tubes that sheltered their inhabitants, much as a raccoon eats a clam after cracking open the mollusk's shell. Moments later, yet another species of fish reminded me of a fisher attacking a porcupine when the fish deftly upended a spiny sea urchin in order to eat its succulent meat without getting stabbed by the victim's prickly defenses.

As I have written in *The Green Trees Beyond*, the sea was almost certainly responsible for my lifetime's interest in the natural world. My fascination began when, as a small child, I strolled into the Mediterranean Sea at the moment when my parents were not watching me and I walked on the sand until my head was below the surface. Keeping my eyes open without suffering more than a slight prickling inflicted by the saline water, and able to see quite well, I spotted a small fish escaping from my clumsy feet. That fish excited me! I had to learn more about its home.

And there is no doubt that the trip I undertook in February 1971, when I sailed for the first time on the Pacific Ocean while exploring British Columbia's Inside Passage in a twenty-four-foot power-boat, was prompted by my coastal and underwater explorations in the Mediterranean Sea and in the Atlantic Ocean. But I also realized later that the death of my wife Joan two years earlier added its own spur to my adventure. Throughout all of 1970, I had been rudderless and extremely restless, unable to find interest in environmental studies. Then, quite suddenly, I became nostalgic for the sea. And I acted.

Four days later I had bought a boat, christened her *The Stella Maris* (The Star of the Sea), and packed her with provisions, plankton nets, a good fishing rod, tackle, an assortment of hooks, and a round net with a stout metal handle. My journey north began in Victoria, British Columbia's capital on Vancouver Island, and did not end until I returned from Ketchikan, Alaska, in October and docked at a Vancouver boat landing.

I have many memories of that fascinating land-and-sea study about which in the future I was to write at length, particularly of a so-called killer whale who came to visit me and my boat one morning in July when I was idling in a cove near the island of Klemtu.

The evening before, seeking to catch a small salmon for my supper, I inadvertently hooked into the mouth of a wolf eel, a creature that was more than six feet long and had a head somewhat like a cantaloupe and a mouthful of fangs. I tried to shake my unwelcome captive off the line for I did not want to kill it and I certainly did not want that creature in my boat. But the fish was evidently caught fast. There was nothing else to do but heave it on board and kill it, which was not an easy task; for some moments, I wondered if the wolf eel was to emerge victorious.

I managed to kill the unfortunate animal, but by then supper time had come and gone and, in truth, I felt considerable remorse.

Settling for a couple of sandwiches and some coffee, I decided while eating that since I knew nothing about my unwanted captive, I would leave its body on the foredeck until the morning, when I would dissect it. I turned in early, tired after my tussle with the unusual creature.

I had intended to lie in, which meant rising at 7:30, but was awakened at 6:00 a.m. by the raucous calls of ravens, seven of which were flying over the *Stella*, undoubtedly preparing to help themselves to parts of the wolf eel. Yawning as I emerged stark naked on the foredeck, I was greeted by a concerto of raven calls and by a few watery droppings that splashed on the deck as the disappointed birds flew off in search of other food. Yawning again, and hoping that the ravens would not return for a time, I had a quick meal that was washed down with water.

By seven o'clock I was ready. Sharp tools in hand, I went forward and began dissecting. But I had only been at the job for about twenty minutes when something near the boat surfaced and heaved a loud breath. Looking up, I met the gaze of a bull orca. He was about ten feet away from the boat and evidently most curious about the object that had "camped" on his domain.

The whale floated calmly, drifting slowly toward me. On impulse, I cut a large chunk of wolf eel and tossed it to my unusual visitor. The huge mouth opened, giving me a brief glimpse of large, yellowish, conical fangs, and the offering was engulfed and swallowed. I tossed him another chunk of fish. That too was swallowed.

I was quite surprised. Orcas do not need handouts from curious biologists. They are more than capable of catching their own breakfast. Was this animal simply being neighborly? Piece by piece I fed Klem, as I was to name him (for the island of Klemtu), the entire wolf eel, the last pieces actually dropping into his cavernous mouth as he "stood on his tail" and whirled upward until his head was just below the rail.

That was a wonderful experience. Klem came to visit the next day, and continued doing so for sixteen days. In between his visits, I would launch my tiny dingy and set out to catch fish — but for the orca, not for me.

During the first week of our friendship, Klem would swim to the boat, puff his somewhat acrid breath, and open his huge mouth, waiting for what I came to think of as his breakfast, although, as I've said, he certainly could have managed to feed himself without my help! But I enjoyed his visits. In truth, however, I was at first somewhat nervous of him — seeing close-up such a huge, carnivorous mammal and to note his large, conical teeth coming to within inches of my reaching hand gave me goose bumps. But not for long, for it quickly became obvious that Klem came in friendship. After the sixteenth visit, Klem came no more. Why he came to visit and to remain that length of time is beyond my imagining, but I was to note later that we had made contact on thirty-seven separate occasions for a total of forty-three hours and seven minutes.

The day before Klem steamed away from my small bay, I dove with him. At first, he appeared to be about to charge me and I thought that my time was up. As he blasted toward me at full speed, all I could see was his big head and the disturbed surface above me. At the very last moment, however, Klem veered away, but his wake tossed me about like a cork. As I recovered, gulped some air from my tanks, and looked for my unorthodox companion, Klem came at me from behind. Again I was tossed around like a cork.

After that, however, my visitor became sedate. He swam around me slowly, narrowing the circle until he was only about ten feet from me, then widening the gap. Then, as my air was getting low, Klem turned and rose to the surface, heading for the open sea. I did not see him again, but he left me an indelible memory of his kind, the so-called killer whales!

The next morning, disappointed by my friend's absence, I landed and started to look for marine specimens in some of the more promising tide pools, which were paradisiacal basins for a curious naturalist.

Soon after paddling along the shallows of a large pool I found a chiton, a mollusk-like inhabitant of coastal waters whose scientific name, *Polyplacophora*, is hardly pronounceable. Chitons are small, oval creatures that feed on minute sea organisms and have been around since the upper Cambrian period, some 570 million years ago. They are about two inches long by somewhat more than an inch wide, and they look very much like a giant pill bug, that tiny creature that resembles a miniature armadillo and can roll up into a ball when disturbed. Then I found a cling-fish, another tide pool denizen. Nature has fitted this little fish with a powerful sucker on its underside. At first, I did not know what it was, but when I put it into my open palm, belly down, to examine it, I discovered that it had sucked itself to my skin. It was neither painful nor strongly adhering, but came away with a soft whoosh when I prized it loose.

I spent all day by, or in, the tide pools and collected and examined more than a hundred creatures I had not seen before. Like land organisms, these animals are connected to each other, whether they are placid grazers that survive on seaweeds, or carnivores that maintain themselves by eating the grazers, protein-rich, minute planktonic organisms, or other carnivores of different species.

As it is on land, everything is, indeed, connected to everything else. The sea is the unifier, with its tides and wind-powered storms that make mountains out of surface waves as they dash to break on the coastlines while yet creating strong undercurrents that cause the death of some organisms, but give food to others — even to those minute beings that, like on the land, burrow beneath the surface. As Emerson wrote: "But in the mud and scum of things / There always, always something sings."

Some twenty-five years ago, I found the skull of a snowshoe hare lying in a small, grassy wilderness opening in northern Ontario during early spring, a time when the buds were just beginning to form on tree and bush branches and the wild grasses had already started poking up out of the soil. As I was to subsequently establish, the animal had been killed, most likely during the previous autumn, by a red fox whose burrow I found not far from the skull's resting place.

By collecting some of the bones that lay at the mouth of the fox den and comparing them with the bleached skull, I was able to determine that the first vertebrae of the spinal column that I had found by the fox's lair fitted exactly into the skull at the appropriate place, leaving no doubt that the remains belonged to the same individual.

The presence of lush green grasses, taller than their more distant neighbors, which grew through the skull's eye sockets as well as immediately around the remains, made it evident that the animal's death had achieved a great deal more than merely to provide food for the predator: it had also supplied nourishment for an indeterminate number of birds, rodents, insects, and soil organisms, and it had released body fluids that had soaked into the soil and enriched it.

The grasses in the area that then grew taller than their

surrounding neighbors owed their vigor to the dead hare's vital fluids — blood and its lymph — that had soaked into the soil. In addition to these local benefits, the hare's death had enriched places farther away through the droppings and urine of the various animals that had consumed some of the hare's parts.

In such ways, the natural world works when left undisturbed by human invasion. It works because it obeys an important law of conservation, which states that nature is careless of the individual, but careful of the species, in this way safeguarding the gene pools of all living things and thus ensuring the continuation of life as we know it today. In effect, this is a fail-safe system that operates through a series of checks and balances that control population numbers over the long term and in accordance with the food resources.

Much is known today about genes and about evolution and much about these two subjects has yet to be discovered, but it is safe to state that if some other "super" species had been present on earth before the advent of modern man and it had behaved as *homo sapiens* has been doing for the past several thousand years, our species would have become extinct, in all probability during the early Stone Age!

Although more living things are produced every year than can be allowed to survive, this is not a wasteful natural practice. Rather, it is wise husbandry of resources. Many of the newcomers — and a number of the old and inefficient — are intended to be the food resources of consumer organisms.

The cycles of life, death, growth, and re-creation go on functioning on a regular basis. On land there are predatory mammals such as the fox that killed the hare; grazing and browsing mammals, such as moose and deer; and rodents, bacteria, slime molds, and fungi; and in the sea, whales and dolphins; sharks and other predatory fish; clams; and mollusks such as octopus and squid — all of these combine to maintain a healthy environment. Within this quite complex scheme, the fittest survive to reproduce, but their numbers vary in accordance with the food resources in ways somewhat reminiscent of the biblical story of the seven fat years being followed by the seven lean years. In nature, however, these periods of feast and famine are not so neatly arranged.

Food, of course, is the burning question, but famine does not usually develop suddenly, nor does it affect all species at the same time. In reality, one, or perhaps several, species of animals and plants begin to decline at a point when those consumers that have been dependent on them have reached maximum population numbers. As food becomes more scarce, overcrowding increases competition for space and nourishment and creates in animals physiological and emotional stress, or, in plants, depletes the soil of needed nutrients and sunshine. In time, depending on the species involved, populations crash dramatically, after which they build up gradually until the cycle is repeated.

Generally, the larger the animal, the longer apart are the peaks and valleys of populations. For example, the time span between moose population highs and lows appears to vary between twenty-five and thirty years, but, depending on the food base, it may fall or rise below or above that figure depending on locations. For the snowshoe hare, the time lapse is between seven and nine years. In the sea, however, such cycles are more difficult to determine, although there is no doubt that they occur naturally. They also happen, of course, when humans interfere with the cycles by overfishing, oil spills, and the introduction of other harmful materials and poisons.

Logically, when prey animal populations crash, predator numbers crash also, but not at once. Rather, they begin to decline from one to several years after the prey's decline. Conversely, in healthy environments, when prey animals increase, their predators will sooner or later increase also.

Some time before committing myself to the study of living things — which is a never-ending occupation — I paid considerable attention to the life cycles that periodically occur worldwide among all species, from amoeba to elephant. That is not to say that I was able to become familiar with all natural cycles. Quite to the contrary! No one person, indeed, not all the biologists in the world, will ever be able to write the definitive history of life cycles, if only because when one cycle is eclipsed, another, probably quite different, arises to take its place. The numbers of life cycles are so numerous that they may be quite endless and thus probably out of the reach of science.

In effect, a life cycle can be defined as a series of developmental changes that are undergone by the individuals that comprise a biological population. Such changes largely depend upon three major biological steps: fertilization, reproduction, and death. As far as we know at present, these cycles have been repeating themselves *ad infinitum*, albeit it is likely that each repetition of a species produces individuals that are somewhat different from their creators in color, shape, and behavior.

So, while studying living things, be these animals or plants, I try to remind myself that it is impossible to fully understand the behavior and characteristics of a species if one ignores the cyclical continuity of life.

During the years that I have studied life in its natural settings, I have learned that the science of biology has a duty to broaden its boundaries and to consciously consider the living organisms that are studied — we must learn to see a mouse, or a lion, or a spider each in its proper perspective, as an integral and essential part of a whole environment. And when we do see things in this way, we should write about our findings in styles that are understandable to the public at large. In other words, those of us who study biology must seek to understand the *personality* of life — not just its mechanics. And we must share with all people the knowledge that we acquire. Only then can we expect to develop the kind of understanding that will fully reconcile the world to the immense value of our natural heritage.

1

Where Eagles Fly

For the first twenty-five miles of my drive from Prince Rupert, which is located on the northern coast of mainland British Columbia, the Skeena River was clear of ice and the snow had melted in the lowland forests. The date was April 5, 1971.

Varied thrushes, juncos, and northern tree sparrows had returned from their southern wintering grounds and bald eagles, in pairs and singly, had been relatively common along my route.

Then, at mile thirty-one by my car's odometer, the first lumps of ice began to appear in the river, their presence suggesting that I was crossing into another biotic zone. The first zone, which I had encountered the previous afternoon soon after I drove off the ferry, had been tempered by the West Wind Drift, or Japan Current; the new zone was created by the cooler air that sweeps down from the tall, ice-covered peaks of the Coast Mountain Range. Precisely where the two zones meet is impossible to tell, but the appearance of ice in the water of the churning river and the patches of snow that still lingered on lowland forest edges suggested the end of one zone and the beginning of the other.

A few miles later I reached the Exchamsiks River and the small campsite that the British Columbia government had created at the point where the smaller stream enters the turbulent Skeena (a site that more recently has been updated as a small provincial park). There, when I stopped the car to look at the scenery, I saw a gathering of eagles. Sliding to the passenger seat and lowering the window, I counted thirty-nine of the big raptors variously located on a stretch of river that was about half a mile long.

The great birds were fishing. Some were flying over the water, others perched in trees or on rocks on both sides of the river's edge. Several had already made strikes and were gulping down their prey. I was so intrigued by the spectacle that I decided to interrupt my journey and stay in the campsite for a few days, or for however long the eagles remained in the area.

Parking the car at the campsite, I took up the binoculars and crossed the road, moving slowly as I reached the river's bank and, where possible, keeping myself behind a screen of shrubs. But I need not have worried. The eagles totally ignored me and continued fishing.

Some minutes later, a female eagle (judged to be so by her large size) braked in mid-air and angled downward, aiming at the water, her legs extended forward and her talons spread. Her action was swift and executed with smooth precision. She hit the river feet first, evidently grabbed something, her body flopping into the water momentarily, and then, her great wings beating rapidly, she flapped upward, spray coming off her wings and body while the talons of her left foot were deeply hooked into the body of a relatively large fish. Rising swiftly, she flew to the far shore.

Landing on a large boulder, the eagle inspected her catch. Through my field glasses I could see that the fish had been already dead when grasped by the bird; otherwise it would have been struggling wildly while it was being taken out of the water and more so when it was dropped on the rock. After a short time I saw that the eagles rising from the river with prey in their claws were all carrying dead fish. Curious, and now ignoring the fact that my presence would probably spook those birds closest to me, I decided to walk down to the river's edge to get a better view. To my surprise, however, the eagles continued catching dead fish. It was as though I was not there!

At the water's edge I was further astonished to see that at least several dozen dead fish were strewn along the sandy shoreline. They were of different species, some only a few inches long, others up to about eighteen inches in length. I felt real concern now, thinking that perhaps some mine a long way upriver might have discharged its effluent directly into the water and poisoned the fish. Presently, however, I noticed a few live fish swimming near the surface about three feet from the riverbank and then I was even more puzzled when I saw that a number of the ice floes that trundled downstream had one or more dead fish lying on top of them. Suddenly, I understood.

It is not uncommon for ice jams to occur in rivers during the start of the spring runoff, when large blocks of ice, downed trees, and other materials are pressed toward a narrow part of a waterway that has already been partly jammed by debris. At some point, as the materials accumulate, they are forced downward, eventually blocking the flow of water. Often, the torrent of icy water flows over the top of the jam, carrying away the detritus and eventually opening the river's course. But on some occasions the ice and debris keep backing up until pressure bursts the dam with an accompanying noise akin to a dynamite explosion. When that happens, logs and rocks and huge pieces of ice are sent downriver, some tumbling wildly on the surface, killing anything in their wake and scouring the bottom of the waterway for some distance.

I had never witnessed such an event, but it was obvious that the eagles, probably accustomed to congregate annually at various sections of rivers that are prone to jamming, were feasting prior to their time of mating.

As I continued to watch the large cakes of ice that were being rafted downriver, I squatted by the water as a male eagle came flapping upstream, flying only about twenty feet above the surface. Just as it went past me, it stooped suddenly, legs extended and claws ready, and a moment later lifted off the water holding a dead fish. Busy watching the bird and about to move my position for a better view, I almost missed seeing a large fish entrapped in a tangle of branches that had accumulated against the shore a few yards from where I squatted.

I retrieved it. It proved to be a humpbacked whitefish (*Coregonus clupeaformis*), a widespread species found in freshwater systems from the Bering Sea to the Labrador coast, as well as in waterways that drain into the Pacific Ocean, the Great Lakes, and even as far south as the Hudson and Susquehanna rivers of the United States.

The specimen I found measured twenty-nine inches in length and weighed fourteen pounds two ounces. Although it had been somewhat mauled by collisions with floating debris, it was still quite fresh.

When I finished examining it, I tossed it as far out into the river as I could manage, watching as it tumbled downstream. It had traveled about fifty yards when one of the eagles that was cruising upriver stooped for it, reaching down with one foot and impaling it, then rising to carry the prize to the top of a tree, there to sit and gorge.

Now, knowing that the eagles were too busy eating to worry about my presence, I spent half an hour walking slowly along the shoreline, stopping often to pick up and examine dead fish. In thirty minutes I pulled fourteen fish out of the shoreline water. One of these was a sculpin (*Myoxocephalus quadricornis*), a common little fish with a large, somewhat flat head and, for its size, huge pectoral fins. Although an adult, it measured three inches. More than twenty freshwater species of sculpins are found in North America and several hundred related species live in the oceans.

The other thirteen fish were boreal smelts (*Osmerus*

eperlanus) that varied in length from eight to eleven inches. These fish are anadromous — they spend their time in the ocean until breeding season approaches, when they migrate up rivers and streams before the ice has broken, a fact that probably accounts for the death of the specimens that I found.

Curious to see if the eagles would accept the fish if they were left on shore, I laid them out on the bank at a location from where I could see them from my nearby camp. By late evening they remained untouched, almost certainly because the eagles were already gorged. But something else took advantage of the fish, although this did not become evident until 2:30 a.m., when a series of loud growls followed by much grunting and snuffling disturbed my sleep and brought me out of my tent, flashlight in hand. Two young bears, two-year-olds by their size, were having an argument over the smelts, a contest that was abruptly terminated by the beam of my lamp.

In the morning the smelts were gone and the human-like footprints of the bears were everywhere along the shoreline and around my tent and around my car, for I had not removed my food from it in order to suspend the attractive edibles from a tree. The gangly twins of last night had scented the food and had circled the car several times. One of them had even climbed on the hood, leaving muddy prints on the windshield. Since I had decided to stay in the campsite for a few days to continue monitoring the eagles, I thought it would be a good idea to find a suitable tree some distance from which I could suspend my food high enough from the ground to be out of reach of bears. But first I had breakfast.

An hour later, with all chores done, I went down to the river to find that twenty-seven eagles had evidently left at first light. But the other twelve birds remained and were hunting when I arrived at the shoreline. Clearly, all the dead fish had been eaten, for the remaining birds were strafing the water in quest of living fish. It was now obvious that the birds were mated pairs. Each couple hunted individually, but remained together when perched in trees and sharing each other's catches; as is normal, the male eagles were about one-quarter smaller than their mates.

Five days after the eagles had nested, I walked to the Skeena to see how the water levels had progressed, but I quickly abandoned that study when I saw a female eagle stoop on a fish, grasp it with one talon, and then try to rise. The catch was evidently too big for the bird! I became alarmed, believing that the eagle would drown. But, to my surprise, the bird simply *rowed* herself ashore, using both wings as sculls and soon gaining the far bank. As soon as she found firm footing, she released her talons at the same time that she stabbed the wriggling fish with her beak. Moments later the fish was dead and she began to tear pieces off it. From my vantage, it appeared that the fish was somewhat more than two feet long and viewed sideways would have been at least six inches deep. I could not identify it conclusively, but I believe it was a northern squawfish (*Ptychpcheilus oregonensis*).

Bald eagles build large, bulky nests in the crowns of dead evergreens, or in deciduous trees. Nests are built with thick branches, the broken-off tips of branches, or twigs. Most of them are lined with deciduous leaves or the tips of conifer needles. The nests are generally used repeatedly and may grow to such proportions that in some cases the top of the nest tree crashes down.

Breeding season in the north starts in late April or early May, depending on locality; in the south eagles breed much earlier, usually in February. As a rule, two eggs are laid, at times only one, rarely, three. Eggs are three inches long and two-and-a-quarter inches across at the widest point. Incubation is usually done by the female alone, although at times both birds take turns.

Between forty-three and fifty-five days later the downy young are born. The eaglets are usually fed by both parents, and they begin to fly between sixty-two and seventy-one days after emerging from the egg.

After the eagle that I then thought of as "the Rower" had evidently taken her fill of squawfish, she left the remains in the tree and flew across the river, passed over my head, and, flying just above the trees, began to call, uttering a fast series of high-pitched, whistling notes.

Moments later, as the big bird disappeared over the evergreens, I heard the relatively distant call of another eagle. Was this the female's partner? I assumed that it was.

On impulse, believing that if I was correct in my assumption the eagles would be nesting in an area that was relatively close to the river — for these great birds rarely breed far from water — I decided to look for the nest. This took all morning and part of the afternoon, but, in the end, led me to the aerie, a huge cup of dead sticks that was lodged in the crown of a massive red cedar, an old tree about 170 feet tall. Perched in the crown of a nearby tree, the male sat very still. It was watching me, but it kept swiveling its head to see what his partner was doing. Then it called, its plaintive whistle causing me to wonder why Nature had given such a small voice to such a big bird.

Watching from a distance of about one hundred yards, I thought it probable that the female eagle had not yet started to lay eggs, but judging by the constant excitement that was soon afterward displayed by both birds, I felt sure that egg laying and nesting would soon take place.

Although I was tempted to spend some time in the vicinity of the nest, I realized that the eagles appeared to be distressed by my presence and were becoming somewhat agitated. Moments later they started calling and soon afterward they began to fly over me, despite the fact that I had sought to camouflage my presence. So, reluctantly, I left the area, allowing the eagles to continue their courtship.

2
An Orphan Bear

Snuffles, a bear cub, came into my life when he was about four months old during a warm day in early June of 1965. I had been walking through a region of forest that backed on to my property and, entering a relatively open area, I was startled by a series of loud, calf-like calls that I recognized as coming from a young bear cub. I knew from experience that the hoarse cries were being uttered in distress.

I stopped to listen, expecting to hear the crashing sounds made by a mother bear running to rescue her cub, but after several minutes, while the calls continued, the surrounding forest was quiet except for the songs of birds. Moving in the direction of the cries, I then noticed three turkey vultures circling over an area about a quarter of a mile from where I was walking.

Now I hurried, convinced that the cub was in real distress, perhaps even injured. At the same time, and although I was determined to rescue the animal if it was in trouble, I remained alert for the sounds of its mother, since sow bears are fierce in the defense of their young.

The distress cries continued intermittently and, after about twenty minutes, the volume of the calls increased, indicating that I was getting close to the animal. Soon afterward I reached an area of large, Cambrian granite boulders. Now the cries were close, obviously on the other side of the rock formation.

I stopped to listen for the approach of the mother bear, feeling decidedly nervous, and singled out a nearby poplar that was large enough to support my weight if I was forced to climb to safety, but that would not support an adult bear.

The cries continued as I waited while expecting at any moment to hear the mother bear, but after about five tense minutes, when nothing untoward occurred, I climbed the rocky escarpment. Looking up, I noted that the vultures were continuing to circle over the area. Then I smelled the stench of rotting meat.

The odor was strong. It suggested that the sow bear was dead and that she had died several days earlier. I hurriedly descended to a small, valley-like place, and presently saw that my guess had been right. The bulk of a large bear sprawled before me. Beside it, cuddled up tightly against the rotting carcass of its mother, was a small cub. Nearby, a second cub lay on its back. It was dead.

As I neared the distressed little survivor, it stopped crying and uttered some pathetic baby snarls, showing its milk teeth and trying to look fierce. Stooping over the cub, I reached out, grabbed him by the scruff of the neck, and brought him up to my body. The cub stank, of course, carrying the odor of its rotting mother. And it was terrified. But, as I hugged it against the left side of my chest, where it would be able to feel the throb of my beating heart, it became quiet. After many years of experience in the rescue of young wild animals, I had expected that close contact with my body and the pulsing beat of my heart would calm the cub.

I started back toward my home, having trouble negotiating the return over the rocky terrain because I had to clasp the cub with one hand. But yet I was pleased that my new ward was quiet. That pleasure, however, ended when the cub clasped my body with both arms, his clutching paws digging sharp little claws into my skin. That worried me, for the cub, which by now I knew to be a male, was covered in his mother's carrion. Would I get an infection? I hurried. The cub continued to clutch me, but he remained quiet.

An hour later I reached home and I carried the little bear into the barn. Then, literally peeling him off my body, I placed him in a straw-filled nesting box that not long before had been the sleeping quarters of two raccoons.

As soon as I put him down, the cub started to cry. But he was too weak to climb out of the box, so I left him, ran to the house, peeled off my shirt so as to attend to the scratches inflicted by the animal's sharp claws, then doused the injuries with strong iodine. Putting on a clean shirt, I next filled two eight-ounce feeding bottles with warm goat's milk, to which I added half a tablespoon of glucose.

Back in the barn, I fed the cub. He quickly emptied both bottles, and wanted more. But I would not allow him to over-feed. I began stroking him as I spoke quietly, and, exhausted as he was, he soon went to sleep.

That day, between early afternoon and ten o'clock at night, the cub ingested six bottles of formula. After the last feed, he went to sleep and soon began to snore.

I spent the night in the barn, alternately lying on an air mattress and sitting up to listen to my new orphan.

At five the next morning, Snuffles awakened me from a nap by calling as loudly as he had been doing when he first came to my attention. As I sat upright, the little bear was starting to climb out of the box, succeeding in squeezing through the opening just as I reached for him. He bit my right hand. But when I put him against my body, he relaxed, so I took him to the house and, working one-handed, I prepared two more bottles of goat's milk formula, having some difficulty doing so because the cub began wriggling just as soon as he scented the food.

By the end of that day, he had relaxed. Now he seemed to look to me as though I were his mother . . . until I took him to the bathroom to wash off the stink that continued to cling to his body. Then he became quite unruly! But three good nips later, with blood flowing from both of my hands, he was clean and fluffed dry and happy to return to the barn, where he began climbing about, exploring, but never losing sight of me.

The next morning, I returned to the dead bear's carcass. The body had been broached by a variety of animals. The stench was now dreadful, but I suspected that the sow had been a casualty of Ontario's iniquitous spring bear hunt; I was determined to do a necropsy on the carcass.

Half an hour later I found the cause of death: a 30.06 caliber bullet lodged in the left lung. Entering, the bullet had broken a rib, one jagged end of which had further lacerated the lung. Evidently the injured sow and her twin cubs had managed to escape into the deep forest. There she had died. After starving for a number of days, one of the cubs, a female, died. Snuffles would not have lasted another twenty-four hours if I had not come upon him.

Before rescuing the cub I had been very much opposed to Ontario's barbaric spring bear hunt. After seeing firsthand the results of such hunting, my opposition grew apace. Today, some thirty years later, I have not been given a reason for changing my mind, especially so because more and more females are being killed by so-called sportsmen who cannot tell the difference between a male and a female bear. Just how many cubs are orphaned and die of starvation each spring after their mothers have been shot cannot be accurately determined.

As matters turned out, the bear became my constant companion for the first two years of his life. He played with me and with my Malamute dog, Tundra, and he often climbed on the roof of the house, there to lounge while leaning against the chimney and, incidentally, to deposit droppings on the shingles.

The last time I saw Snuffles was in September of 1969,

three months after my wife, Joan, had died from a brain hemorrhage.

I was outside the house, and I had just finished packing my car, preparing to sell the property, when the bear emerged from a cedar thicket and ambled toward me. As usual, I had a pocket full of peanuts and as Snuffles came closer, I offered him a shelled nut. He took it, his prehensile lips lapping it off my opened hand; then he ate it daintily, as usual. I was again reminded of the many occasions he had come to our home, as an adult, to stand by the kitchen window and grunt until Joan or I would open the glass and give him a peanut-butter sandwich. Always he was gentle; always he grunted softly after he had eaten his snacks. Yet he invariably ran off to hide if we had visitors.

Now, knowing that this would be the last time that I saw my shaggy, gentle friend, I kept feeding him peanuts until my pocket was empty. Then, entering the house, I returned with a rather stale sponge cake, a large one. As I offered it to him, I spoke:

"That's my good-bye snack, Snuffles. Now we are both on our own."

Some moments later we parted. Snuffles entered the forest; I entered my car and drove away, never to return.

3
The Carrion Eaters

One morning in early June 1968, while I was walking through a wilderness region that lies about 150 miles north of Toronto, in south central Ontario, and as I began to climb up a rather crumbled rock face, a relic of the Cambrian period that thrust itself in my path, I was suddenly assailed by a very strong smell. The odor was not unfamiliar to me; it was the effluvium given off by putrefying meat.

For me, wilderness smells are all interesting, whether they are pleasant or otherwise, for every detectable odor carries a message, albeit some smells are hard to read. So when my nose is suddenly filled with a good, ripe aroma, I usually allow it to lead me to the source. I continued to climb.

When I reached the top of the scarp, the odor became stronger, but at first I could not locate its source. Some moments later, however, as I stood scanning the area, I heard a strange, relatively quiet noise, something between a hiss and the sound of a person clearing his throat. I stood still, feeling sure that the sound had come from a place where a slab of rock had at some time fallen against a large boulder, creating a sort of lean-to effect. Next I heard a brief rustling noise. I was right — the soft shuffling noise had come from beneath the leaning rock slab.

I moved ahead slowly and breathed through my mouth to try to reduce some of the smell that was now strong in the area. It took me a couple of minutes to reach the source of the smell. I lowered myself to my haunches and peered into the cave-like space.

Inside, to my amazement, crouched a large black bird with a red and naked head, a turkey vulture (*Cathartes aura*). Beside the bird lay two lumps that were covered in long down and were of a cream-to-light buff color. The stench that emanated from the vulture nest cannot be accurately described! Nevertheless, despite the nauseating stench, I was determined to see more of the twin lumps, which were, of course, vulture chicks hiding their heads under themselves.

At first, I confess, I was somewhat fearful of the hen vulture. As near as I could estimate, she stood slightly less than two feet, with her head almost touching the narrowest part of the rock slab where it made contact with the boulder. She continued to stand erect and unmoving, but she kept her jet black, shiny eyes fixed on me and on my every movement. I stared at her feathers, as black as an undertaker's livery; at her red head, with its half-circle of wrinkled white under each eye; and, especially, at the huge, heavy, and sharply curved beak, the last third of which was ivory white. Would she attack if I tried to lift up one of her young?

Uncomfortably, I recalled the times that I had seen through field glasses the ways in which vultures ripped meat off dead animals, and although thus far the bird had shown absolutely no aggression, that sharp point of her beak was definitely intimidating. Yet I desperately wanted to get a look at one of her chicks!

I moved closer, stopping when I was about three feet away from the shelter. But now, since I was higher than the rocky nest, I could not see into it. I crouched. I was still unable to look into the grotto, so I kneeled down and sat on my legs. Now I could look right inside. The vulture remained unmoving. Hesitantly, I reached in, my hand open and held upward, my eyes glued to the unwavering gaze of the vulture's black orbs. But she did not move.

I lowered my hand slowly, reaching farther in; turning the palm down, I laid it on the nearest vulture chick. The hen's eyes followed my hand, but she did not move. Emboldened, I slid my hand under the belly of the nearest chick. It was warm and smooth, the natal down feeling smooth. As I began to lift the chick, it raised its head. It was undoubtedly the ugliest young creature I had ever seen. Although its birth coat was far from ugly, its dark gray head and staring eyes seemed to belong to a prehistoric creature.

Not wanting to unduly disturb the hen and her offspring, I put the chick back in its place, whereupon it immediately hid its head back under its body. Then, as I was withdrawing my hand, I paused on impulse and reached toward the hen. She remained immobile. Gently, I stroked her left wing. She stayed still, but now her eyes followed my hand.

As I was getting to my feet, the horrendous odor of carrion assaulted me anew. In my excitement, I had actually inhaled the smell, but I had not given it conscious thought. Walking backward, away from the crude "nest," I lifted my hand and was about to sniff at it to see if the chick had reeked as much as its mother and its nesting quarters. Before my hand was halfway up to my nose, I had the answer: I smelled like a vulture!

As that thought entered my mind, I was startled by what sounded like the rattle of a number of dry sticks. Looking up, I was in time to see the splendid six-foot wings of the male vulture as it swooped down and glided over the trees, its feather shafts quivering and creating the rattling. But then, because it is almost impossible to distinguish between male and female vultures, it may have been the female sailing over me and the bird in the nest may have been the male!

Years before that encounter, when discussing bird behavior with an ornithologist of my acquaintance, he had told me that nesting vultures are almost impossible to chase off their nests. I had not paid much attention to his comment. (If you happen to read this, Bob, accept my apologies for doubting your words!)

The breeding times of turkey vultures vary according to latitude. In the north breeding begins about mid-April and in the south it starts in January. Females and males take turns incubating the sub-elliptical eggs, which are two-and-three-quarter inches long by almost two inches long at their widest part. Incubation varies between thirty-eight and forty-one days, and the young begin to fly short distances about ten weeks after emerging from the eggs. Two eggs are usual, but one or three are sometimes laid.

Turkey vultures are found from southern Canada to Mexico and other regions in Central America. Occasionally, one or more of these birds may stray as far north as the Yukon Territory. At least two such occurrences were noted in the gold mining region of the territory during the 1930s. One of these vultures was shot and photographed in Dawson.

While driving through southeastern Texas in 1960, I was greatly impressed with the black vultures (*Caragyps atratus*), which, as I was approaching the Rio Grande, seemed to be lining both sides of the arrow-straight highway over which I had already noted a veritable plethora of large hunting spiders.

Intrigued by the vultures, I stopped a number of times to watch them, admiring their stately, jet-black plumage, the equally black, naked, and wrinkled heads, and the ebony beaks, the tips of which are an off-white hue.

The birds were not a bit afraid of me. I was able to get close enough to several of them as they sat on the edge of the road, or perched in seemingly dead and stark honey mesquite trees (*Prosopis glandulosa*), skeletal shapes anchored in the dry areas on the west side of the highway.

Those vultures had plenty of carrion! It seemed to me that about every mile or so of highway there were two or three dead armadillos, which had been killed by traffic. Confirming the vulture's reputation for actually attacking and killing small mammals, I twice saw two single birds swoop down and kill half-grown armadillos. On each occasion, other vultures swooped down to "help" the hunter eat the food.

Like its red-headed relative, the black vulture usually lays two eggs, but may produce only one or, exceptionally, three. The eggs are larger than those of the turkey vulture, measuring almost three inches in length and two inches in width. Incubation is shared by both sexes and lasts thirty-eight to forty-one days.

Black vulture chicks are almost fully grown by the time they are six weeks old, but although some feathers have appeared by then, their coats of down are still present. Eleven weeks after hatching, the young blacks begin to fly, but they are not yet as graceful as their soaring parents.

Vultures have interested me ever since I saw and studied the huge birds that clean up the carrion on the plains of East Africa. I especially remember a day I spent watching the behavior of Africa's white-backed vultures, which rarely feed anywhere except on rotting carcasses. These large scavengers have long, naked, reddish-skinned necks and massive, curved black beaks, a combination that allows them to reach deep into the carcass of a dead wildebeest or zebra and gorge on the tender entrails. In one case, I watched a vulture open the putrefying stomach of a dead zebra and actually climb inside the carcass, from where it was only dislodged by the arrival of half a dozen other birds of its kind.

During the time I spent watching the Texas black vultures,

I compared their behavior with that of the white-backed vulture. The African bird is considerably larger than its American counterpart, and, of course, the white-backed scavenger usually feeds on the carcasses of large animals. By comparison, I thought as I watched two black vultures fighting over the carcass of one dead armadillo, the Texas birds had to work a lot harder in order to keep themselves fed. In fact, the Texas vultures reminded me of their European counterparts, which are also black and must also survive on small dead animals. It was the European species that first attracted me to these useful birds, which I noticed in Spain's Pyrenean mountains when I was twelve years old.

As I drove south after observing the graceful Texas scavengers for about five hours, I once again thought about the cyclical continuity of life, particularly as it applies to the *enormous* vultures whose skeletons were found in the La Brea Tar Pits that are today flanked by Wiltshire Boulevard of Los Angeles, California. These vultures, the wings of which spanned twelve feet, have been named *Teratornis* (monster bird) and they are thought to have existed some time during the Pleistocene period, which lasted about one million years. Eventually, however, *Teratornis*' cycle ended and the new cycle gave rise to the next largest bird known, the California condor, which has a wingspan of some nine feet. This bird is, incidentally, threatened with extinction due to hunting, poisoning of carcasses, and destruction of habitat.

Such thoughts occupied me for the remainder of that day and on into late evening during a meal in Monterrey, Mexico.

4
Slip and Slide

A number of years ago I received a frantic telephone call from a woman in the Whitby, Ontario, area asking me to help her catch two otters and remove them from her home.

"Please! I need help. Joe, my husband, is in hospital — they bit him something awful . . ."

When I had succeeded in calming her down, I wanted to know how two otters had entered a home that was miles away from water, the usual habitat of these large members of the weasel family.

It turned out that the couple, believing that owning exotic pets would boost their image, had read an advertisement from a U.S. animal breeder who was offering otters at $200 each. The advertisement, as I recall it, went something like this: "Young otters make ideal pets. We have a few left from our latest litter. Only $200 each. You pay shipping costs. We furnish health papers, crating, and transport to airport."

The foolish buyers sent off a check in payment, booked cargo space on an aircraft, and, when notified of the arrival of their "babies," as they called them before seeing them, dashed to Toronto Airport and claimed their exotic pets, both of whom arrived in the same wooden crate. They were so cramped for space that they could hardly turn around.

The drive home was anxious! The captives voiced their distress with shrill, whistle-like cries, which were ear-piercing in the closed vehicle, despite the whirring of the air conditioner. Occasionally, grunt-like growls and hisses interrupted the whistling and bad odors began to assail the nostrils of the proud owners — otters, like all weasels, have strong-smelling musk that is discharged when they are upset or aggressive.

Finally, some two hours after they had taken charge of the crate, the couple reached home. Anxious to release their "babies," Joe dashed down to the basement and rushed back with a flat pry-bar and a hammer.

Watched by his impatient wife, Joe attacked the crate, hammering the flat bar between the lid and the sides and prying upward. The hammering, the shriek of nails coming loose, and the excited babble of the happy couple greeted two husky, almost full-grown otters as the lid parted company with the crate. Out they came, agile, dirty, and very angry. Joe tried to catch one — the biggest, a male — and was instantly rewarded with two bites: one in the fleshy web between thumb and forefinger, which penetrated right through, and one on his right wrist, a slashing bite that bled profusely.

The couple was shocked! The otters were almost four feet long from nose to end of tail and were as supple and swift as quicksilver. Before Joe could do more than yell his anguish, and before his wife could jump back to avoid the female otter, who, ivory-teeth bared, had sprung toward her, the "exotic pets" disappeared from the kitchen.

After about twenty minutes — the time it took to disinfect and bind Joe's wounds — an otter hunt began.

Joe had left the basement door open when he returned with the liberating tools. And his wife, who had used the bathroom, had failed to close the door and had left the toilet seat cover in the upright position. When the animals were released, the female raced for the basement, while the male took refuge in the bathroom, where he soon found the toilet and the only water around. In a thrice, the otter jumped into the refuge. Sitting upright in the bowl, he greeted Joe with his mouthful of powerful teeth as the wounded, would-be exotic pet owner entered and sought to recapture the escapee, perhaps feeling brave because he had donned a pair of stout leather gloves.

The woman, meanwhile, had gone down to the basement, but she had hardly set foot in the toolroom when the otter, clicking her teeth and hissing, charged her. The woman fled upstairs and slammed the basement door.

Moments later Joe emerged from the bathroom, this time bleeding from a deep, tearing bite on his left forearm, another on the back of his right hand, and deep puncture wounds high up on his thigh, close to his right groin, and, as he was to note later, "near my manhood." He had foolishly decided that he could use a folded bath towel to cast over the otter so that he could grab him without getting bitten — he had not, however, I was to learn, decided what he would do with the animal if he managed to catch him once it was wrapped in the towel! In any event, Joe miscalculated.

Otters are lithe and sinuous. Soaking otters are harder to grip than a wet cake of bath soap. The frantic animal bit wrist and hand almost simultaneously, squirmed out of the towel, and bit Joe's groin area on his way down. On touching the carpeted floor, the captive returned to the toilet bowl in a swift blur, from whence he continued to hiss at the retreating "exotic pet" owner.

Joe had to go to hospital to get his wounds stitched, to get anti-tetanus shots, and to be scared half to death when a well-meaning doctor suggested that it would be necessary to give Joe a series of rabies inoculations if the otter turned out to be rabid.

In those days I traveled with several sizes of live-traps in my station wagon, so I was able to remove both otters from the home of their owners, but not until three o'clock the following morning. I caught the female first and easily by enticing her into the trap with a plateful of canned sardines — she was starving; the otters had not eaten since the previous day.

The male was somewhat more recalcitrant, albeit he allowed me to perch on the edge of the bathtub and seemed to pay attention to my voice, if not to my actual words, as I quietly talked nonsense to him. Finally, tempted by the odor of sardines, he emerged dripping from the toilet and entered the live trap.

I guaranteed to quarantine the two animals for three months in case of rabies — I was sure that they were healthy, just simply good and angry — by which time Slip, the male, and Slide, the female, as I had named them, ate out of my hand and followed me when I took them for walks to our local pond.

During their play time at our pond, Slip and Slide alternated between swimming and diving — when they caught fish — and chasing each other along the shoreline; at times Slide was the chaser, then Slip would take on the role. Their frolics were always energetic, but stopped as soon they heard a hawk's shrill hunting cry, at which time they would dash to me and climb on my person. This was an event I did not enjoy for they were always soaking wet. I was also concerned about predators, and I visualized a time when they would be released and so be on their own. Under such conditions they would not have me as their protector.

So, after some trouble, I managed to teach the two rambunctious animals to dash into the shrubbery when they felt threatened, but in the end I need not have worried. By the following spring, when they were one year old and released on our property, they had responded to their biological needs and behavior and were quite capable of killing any hawk that might have been foolish enough to dare their sharp teeth and the speed at which they could use them.

With me, however, they were always gentle and responded when I called them, even after they had been released on a large, unnamed lake, a corner of which abutted on our 350-acre wilderness property. There they remained happily until the following spring, when Slip traveled across country to another lake and Slide mated with a local male. (Male otters are not ready to breed successfully until they are five or six years old, while females are sexually mature during the second year of life. This arrangement is nature's way of limiting brother–sister matings.)

River otters, as they are called to distinguish them from sea otters, are found across Canada, being absent only from the prairies and the extreme north. The third largest member of the weasel family, next to the wolverine and the badger, an adult male otter will measure almost five feet in length from nose to end of tail and will weigh up to thirty pounds — females are about twenty percent smaller and lighter.

Like weasels, after a female has mated, the fertilized eggs undergo what may be termed "suspended animation," not developing further until the following spring. This means that from the time of mating, which varies among females, pregnancy can last from about nine months to almost thirteen months. This arrangement is beneficial to otters and members of this family because the winter months are hard on the animals and developing young within the female would steal too much energy from her. In all likelihood, neither the mother nor the litter would survive a northern North American winter.

River otters are stealthy wilderness dwellers. They can occasionally be seen in daylight, but are more likely to be active during evening, night, and early morning. Family oriented and playful, otters love to slide, in winter using a snowbank that slopes to lake ice, and in summer a muddy slope that ends in a plunge into clear water. At a fast clip, on land, otters can travel at about eighteen miles an hour.

Otters feed on fish (catfish, perch, rock bass, and other species), crayfish, clams, frogs and newts, and a variety of insects. Most of their food is taken under the water, in which they are very much at home.

Typical otter habitats are clear lakes, rivers, large and deep beaver ponds, and clean marshes. From spring to autumn, because of disturbance by motorboats, otters are rare on large lakes.

As matters turned out, Slip seemed to be quite happy in and around his new lake, even to the point where he ignored me when I went to visit him. He knew who I was (I could tell by the fact that he did not run away from me), but although he would pass within three or four feet when I happened to be standing on the shoreline, he only dignified my presence with a sideways look. I was pleased by such behavior, for I did not want him to trust other humans.

Slide, on the other hand, despite having mated and rearing three kittens, never broke our bond, although she kept her young away from me. The male, her husband, a fully wild otter, of course, invariably disappeared when I arrived. But Slide, just as invariably, came skipping toward me and nothing would do but that I pat her head. That seemed to satisfy her, for she would immediately return to the lake and to her young.

She did, however, eventually return to the wild, but it took almost six years for her to do so.

5
The Ravens

The start of British Columbia's Nass River lies approximately two hundred miles — as the raven flies — south of the Yukon Territory. The birthplace of the long winding river is not much to look at. It is quite a swampy area that feeds a relatively small lake, which in turn feeds the budding Nass. These waterways are fed by the spring snow melt, as well as by the summer tears of the mountain peaks. As it gathers more and more meltwater, the Nass widens and becomes deeper, trundling frothily and noisily through the spectacular canyons that are periodically encountered amid the river's rugged forest valleys and natural meadows, all of which are typical of the country that lies east of the Coast Mountain Range.

In the early 1970s I spent a number of months in that region's wilderness, studying the general environment but more particularly mountain lions, wolves, and ravens. I have written about some of my adventures in that region, but because of the volume of fascinating animals, plants, waterways, and mountains to be found there, I have not described many of the events and experiences recorded in my notebooks.

The story of the ravens and the wolves, although briefly mentioned here and there in some of my works, has not been properly recorded, yet I believe it is worth the telling. The wolves, however, who must surely be my alter egos, played a secondary role in the events in mid-July of 1970 that transpired in a valley near the source of the Nass River.

It was early afternoon. I had climbed up to about the two-hundred-foot level of the eastern face of one of the many unnamed mountains so as to look into the valley where I had pitched my tent a week earlier. Sitting on a boulder behind a screen of white spruce seedlings, I observed through field glasses a pack of eight wolves. They were trotting along a communicating valley that runs between Mount Beirnes and Devil's Claw Mountain, and moving in a westerly direction. Earlier, as I scanned the area where the narrow valley meets one of the wider valleys of the Nass River, and about a mile ahead of the pack, I had seen an obviously aging mule deer buck that was walking — almost staggering — toward the river.

While watching the wolves, I had, of course, lost sight of the mule deer, but when I moved my focus from the wolves to the buck, I was just in time to see him stumble and then go down, his front legs sticking out straight ahead and his back legs tucked under his haunches. A moment later his head drooped, then it fell to lie cheek-down on the grass. Through the binoculars I could see that he was gasping for breath. It was obvious that he was moribund.

Now I heard the voices of the ravens. Earlier, seven of the big black birds had been sitting high in the trees, a vantage that obviously allowed them to keep sight of the deer. When the buck collapsed, the ravens began to call, uttering loud, excited cawings, cacklings, whistlings, and cooings while flying from tree to tree. Every now and then one or two of the birds dove downward to land within a few feet of the moribund old buck. Then, having carefully inspected the animal, they alternately walked and hopped closer to him, each bird uttering even louder calls that were soon repeated by the other birds.

I had seen that kind of drama before. The deer was obviously on its last legs and the ravens knew it. As I was about to search for the wolves, eight more ravens arrived, swelling the total to fifteen, some of the newcomers landing near the deer, others joining their companions in the trees.

Focusing the binoculars, I soon relocated the wolves. They continued to trot; their gait was steady, and none of the pack members showed excitement. Yet, judging from the manner in which from time to time they had earlier raised their noses to sniff the air, it was obvious that they had detected the deer soon after I had first seen them, probably while they were still more than a mile away.

Now, it has often been said that ravens deliberately lead wolves to healthy prey, and such comments suggest that there is a compact between wolf and raven. This is not so. In the first place, ravens do not congregate in trees above healthy, active deer, or other ungulates, albeit that a few of the big black birds may follow one or more moose or caribou in order to swoop down on the animal's excrement, the oblong, brown droppings that either form a small pile when the animal stops to defecate, or become a scattering of pellets if the animal defecates on the move. In any case, ravens will descend on the droppings and spread them apart with their beaks and then ingest whatever bits of protein they can find. Ravens do this to the excrement of any large mammal, especially that of bears during the summer, for such droppings contain many undigested seeds as well as numbers of parasitic worms and larvae. But in such situations, the ravens do not congregate, perhaps dropping on the fecal material in ones or twos and soon after soaring upward in search of other foods.

If a pack happens to be relatively nearby when one or more ravens stop for such a snack, the wolves may lope toward the location, although they immediately abandon the search if the birds rise into the trees, or fly away, for such behavior immediately tells the predators that the birds have landed for a mere snack. If, however, the ravens encounter a dead or dying animal, they immediately become excited, cawing and whistling and, in fact, delivering a noisy cacophony that advertises either the presence of actual food or a dying animal.

Upon hearing the calls, other ravens race to the location. So do such birds as gray jays, woodpeckers, and chickadees, as well as mice and shrews and squirrels. The lesser birds perch in the trees and wait their turn; the mice and shrews and squirrels hide in the nearby underbrush. (The small creatures of the wilderness are well aware that ravens, apart from being opportunistic scavengers, are also avid hunters of small birds and mammals.) Nevertheless, the small fry know that after the ravens have finished their feast, there will be many crumbs left for them.

If an animal is already dead when found by the ravens, their excitement rises and they descend on the carcass. However, it is not unusual for the big black birds to waste time sparring with each other, engaging in noisy, but rather harmless skirmishes that are sure to attract a wolf pack if these animals are within two or three miles of the rowdy event.

Wolves know full well that when ravens congregate, they are most probably either waiting for a sick or aged animal to die, or they are arguing over the remains of a dead animal. Under such conditions, the wolf leaders steer the pack to the ravens and, if the prize is worth it, the wolves will settle down to eat. At first the ravens fly up into nearby trees, cawing and screeching. But just as soon as they see that the wolves have become fully occupied with their meal, they fly down and virtually surround the pack, walking and hopping and voicing their disappointment while watching closely, waiting for a chance to pick up an unguarded piece of meat, or a bone.

In fact, as I have observed a number of times, ravens, working cooperatively, will deliberately taunt the wolves, one bird seeking to distract, while another will hop in and grab a piece of meat. In some instances a raven may walk to the rear of a feeding wolf and pull its tail! The intent is to distract a wolf, but the ruse only works with young, inexperienced wolves —

a veteran pack member simply ignores the tugs, even when a raven pulls the tail four or five times before giving up. But a young wolf will often jump up and swing around to try to catch the offending bird. While it is so engaged, another raven will swoop down and steal the youngster's food! After that, the instigator of the action rises swiftly and pursues the bird that has escaped with the food.

Such behavior is not consciously cooperative; nevertheless the birds do work in unison and as often as not the raven that has got away with the prize will on some other occasion distract a wolf while its mate, or a member of the loosely knit group, gets away with the food.

There can be no doubt that ravens are highly intelligent and quick to take advantage of anything that they foresee is to their benefit. And they are good learners, as my wife, Sharon, discovered during the summer of 1976 in Watson Lake, Yukon Territory.

Soon after we had settled ourselves in the town and I was putting the finishing touches to my new office, my wife had gone shopping. On her return, after storing the groceries, she came to my room.

"Why do so many Yukoners have tame ravens? And how is it that the birds are happy to ride in the back of half-ton trucks?" she asked.

At first I was a little taken aback by the questions, then I realized that she had seen what is a common sight in the north: opportunistic ravens riding in the back of pick-up trucks that are heading for town. The ravens are totally wild, but they evidently learned some years ago that wherever there are communities in the north, there are garbage bags replete with good things to eat! So, saving their energy, they hitch morning rides in the boxes of trucks, most of which are usually crammed with old tires and other impedimenta, which give the birds good footholds. Arriving in town, the ravens fly away immediately and go to work on any plastic garbage bags that have been left outside!

At first, Sharon believed that I was pulling her leg, but the next morning, walking up to the Alaska Highway, she monitored the arrival of the hitch-hiking ravens and watched as one by one they left the trucks on which they had arrived and flew off in search of food. Throughout the north, hitch-hiking ravens are a common sight, as any Yukoner or Alaskan will confirm.

Later that year, while I was writing at my desk at the back of the house, I became disturbed by a monotonous, metallic banging from somewhere in front of the house. I tried to ignore it at first, but after several minutes I got up and went to the front room window.

A large raven was perched on the top board of a garbage-can container that I had built to keep the roaming dogs away from our metal cans. The six-by-four-foot slatted container sat on two-foot-high legs, so I had believed that our garbage would remain in place until it was time to go to the local dump. But I had not reckoned with the ravens, or, at least, with that particular bird.

From its wooden perch, the bird bobbed forward and thrust its head down, grabbed the handle of the garbage-can lid with its beak, pulled upward, and let go. The lid fell with a clatter and jumped up and down a couple of times, but it did not come off. As soon as the lid settled, the bird repeated the performance.

As I watched, I grinned facetiously, believing that there was no way that the bird could remove the can's lid. Watching it work and also keeping my eye on about six of its peers that sat in a nearby tree, I admired the raven's ingenuity and dedication. I was almost sorry that its efforts would fail. I should have known better!

I didn't count the number of bounces inflicted on the can's lid by the raven, but I would guess that the bird must have lifted the lid about twenty times before it did, indeed, bounce off. I was amazed! But more was to follow.

The raven, maintaining its perch on the uppermost board of the garbage-can cage, then pulled aside the loose lid and dipped its head and neck into the can. It pulled out a paper bag.

Now, holding the bag in its beak, the bird flew off the can and soared upward. Roughly thirty feet from the ground, it dropped the bag much as a war-time aircraft might release a bomb. The impact on the driveway burst the bag and spilled the contents: the fried chicken remains of our previous evening's supper. The raven flew down and grabbed a drumstick to which much skin and some meat adhered, then its companions landed and helped themselves as the originator of the feast flew into a tree and devoured its prize.

Bird books refer to this remarkable avian as the common raven, but there is nothing "common" about *Corvus corax*.

Why, then, use such an adjective? I can only assume that naturalist John James Audubon, or whoever first gave the raven its English name, meant "widespread," for this large, shiny, black bird is, indeed, widespread, earning its living in both the New and Old worlds and ranging from the High Arctic across Canada — except the open prairies, which have no trees — and Alaska, south through the western United States and Mexico, to Nicaragua and eastern North America, to northern Michigan, Minnesota, Maine, the Appalachian Mountains, and south to the northern regions of Georgia. In the eastern hemisphere, *Corvus* is found from northern Eurasia to North Africa, northwest India, Japan, and Asia Minor.

Observed when flying high, or when sitting quietly in shadowy places, the raven's feathers appear to be sooty black; but when the sun glances off the plumage it elicits alternating light violet and deep purple shades. At one moment an observer is charmed by the purple glow, and at the next by the gentle violet hues; at times, when sunlight strikes a folded wing, its feathers seem to reflect, giving off a mirror-like flash.

Seen in profile, there is no mistaking the heavy, black beak that tapers to a hooked point, a business-like tool that may be used as a weapon of defense, or as a means of killing prey, or for tearing meat off the remnants of the kill made by a wolf, bear, or mountain lion.

Although most of its plumage is sleek and tidy, the raven has what can only be described as a beard. This begins at the underside of the beak, at its base, from where the down-sloping feathers stick out and, when seen against the light, show a thick cluster of downward pointed pennae that push away slightly from the bird's neck.

I have always thought that ravens are ventriloquists since they have a great variety of calls, some of which, I am sure, are copied from the calls of other birds. During the winter of 1959, while walking through the boreal forest in the Yukon Territory, I heard a variety of tree-top calls that I could not identify; nor, on looking up, could I find the originator of the cacophony. At one moment calls sounded almost like the mewling of a kitten, at the next they became deeper, then harsh and raucous, and then cooing.

It was a repertoire unlike anything I had ever heard, but I eventually spotted the noise maker: a large raven sitting on a branch. It was almost unmoving, its head up, its throat quivering, and its beak opening and closing rapidly with a castanet-like rhythm. When the bird noticed that I was watching, it began to caw and moments later nine more ravens appeared to combine their voices into what I felt was a series of arias, going from bass to alto while each singer fluffed its feathers.

Later that day, when I was walking along a game trail that was almost arrowstraight and quite wide, I saw two ravens on the snow. They were a courting pair. I stopped at once, expecting the birds to fly away, but, although they had obviously seen me, they paid me little attention. The male, recognized by his larger size, was literally dancing, first on one foot, then on the other, while he fluffed out his feathers and bowed and cooed, his antics taking him right around the hen, who stood quietly, but with feathers also fluffed out, while she watched her mate's nuptial dance.

In North America, ravens breed between February and early March in the south and from about mid-March to mid-April in the north. Where there are rocky outcrops, ravens will use these as their nesting site provided the location is sheltered; in the forests they usually nest in evergreen trees such as spruces, pines, and larches.

Raven nests are large, consisting of a mass of sticks and twigs woven together with a variety of plant materials that are combined with damp earth and mosses. The nesting cup is first lined with grasses, next with deciduous leaves and mosses, then further lined with animal fur and hair. Both birds contribute to the nest's construction, but the female incubates on her own after she has laid between three and seven eggs — usually four to six. The eggs are sub-elliptical in shape and quite large, usually one-and-three-quarter inches long by one-and-a-quarter wide. Markings are extremely variable and decorated by spots, or streaks of light olive, dark or olive brown, and dark gray. The female lays her eggs at intervals of one to two days. While she is incubating she is fed by her partner, who works hard to keep his mate well fed during the twenty to twenty-one days that it takes for the chicks to be born. Both parents feed the young, which learn to fly after about six weeks.

My first experience of North American ravens took place in 1954, when I was a neophyte homesteader in Ontario. Since then, during the last forty-one years, I have continued to be captivated by these ebony opportunists.

Today, as I write, a flock of about twenty ravens are waiting in the surrounding forest for the handouts that we put out daily in an area near our home. As usual they are early. It is now two o'clock, and we distribute the food in the evening. But they sing and talk as they wait patiently, and we always enjoy their company. They are our friends.

6
Humans and Wolves

My first encounter with free-ranging wolves occurred one January morning in 1955, at a time when I was cutting pulpwood to earn a meager living that allowed me to remain in a wilderness region to do field studies. I had been in Canada since June of the previous year and a scant five weeks in the boreal forests of northwestern Ontario.

As had already become my habit, I set out for my four-mile-distant cutting site an hour before sunrise, tramping along the trail that my snowshoes had made two weeks earlier in the three-foot-deep snow. En route, about two miles from my objective, my nearest neighbor, Harold Hanson, was already getting ready to cut black spruces when I stopped to chat with him. During our brief conversation I noted that he had brought his 30.30 rifle with him and I asked him why he had done so.

"Moose time." The laconic reply was delivered with a strong Norwegian accent.

January was a long way from the legal hunting system, but the scattered homesteaders who lived in the area hunted for meat about three times each winter, since the nearest source of "boughten gru" was twenty-nine miles away. Technically they were poachers. In fact, they were survivors. They had to hunt to live.

I left Harold's camp and trudged along, arriving at my cutting site as the sun was peeping above the trees. There, I hung my food bag on a tree, picked up axe and four-foot bow saw, and selected a ten-inch-wide black spruce. I had just axed the required notch in the fall-side of the tree trunk and was about to pick up the saw when the wolves arrived.

I heard the sounds they made as they approached. Then, as they all began to howl-bark while running around me, I froze, feeling the paralysis of fear. For some moments I remained crouched by the tree, saw in hand, but when I caught sight of two of the marauders — large, brownish-and-white animals — I stood upright, picked up the axe, and backed toward the four-foot-high pile of cut pulpwood that was about twenty feet away.

The wolves continued to howl-bark and run around me. I could only catch fleeting glimpses of one or another of them. Yet, they did not seem to be tightening their circle. But I was still fearful.

After a childhood during which I played with wild animals,

including small sharks, and later, as an adult, after studying biology at Cambridge University in England, and doing field studies of carnivores in Africa, when I landed in Canada in 1954 I was under the impression that I had long ago learned to ignore mythology and instead to believe only those things that were supported by irrefutable evidence. I also firmly believed that I was not afraid of any wild animal.

Nevertheless, finding myself surrounded by the vociferous wolves, I succumbed to fear, replaying in my mind the many mythological stories that even today continue to depict the wolf as a killer of humans.

At the log pile, I added a four-foot pole to my puny armament and, trying to keep turning to face the circling pack, I prepared to defend myself while firmly believing that I was sooner or later going to be killed and probably eaten.

After a time, however, while the wolves continued their circling and howling, I could no longer stand the uncertainty.

With my weapons at the ready, I left the wood pile, walked to my trail, and started out on it, without snowshoes. Stumbling through the snow, I headed for my neighbor. I was hoping to borrow his rifle so that I could return and, if the wolves were still around, exact vengeance on them for the fear that they had caused me.

Resisting the temptation to look back, I trudged along as fast as I could without allowing myself to panic, but after about five or six minutes, with the wolf howls still filling the forest, I stopped and looked back at my trail. It was empty. Listening more intently, it seemed to me that the howls were now more distant.

I reached Harold Hanson without mishap, borrowed his rifle and ten cartridges, and loaded the weapon. My neighbor grinned and told me that wolves did not attack people, but I returned to my trail more determined than ever to exact vengeance on the wolf pack if it was still around.

When I reached my logging site all was quiet. Advancing toward the log pile I noticed that one or more wolves had urinated on my bow saw. They had also marked my log pile at various places. Then I saw blood on the snow, a streak of it. I walked toward the red mark and noted that it had been put there by a paw. Advancing further, I soon discovered why the wolves had howl-barked at me until I had left the area. The pack had made a kill. I must have arrived just in time to disturb them while they were eating.

Apart from being annoyed with myself for allowing fear to cloud my reason, I felt stupid. No wonder Harold had grinned at me when he lent me his gun! He'd lived in the area for some thirty years, soon after he had arrived in Canada as an immigrant, and, as he told me later, he had never been so much as threatened by wolves or by any other animals, including bears.

One week later, when I was heading home from another part of the wilderness, having spent the day making an inventory of tree species, I sensed that I was being followed. This time, however, there was no fear, merely eager curiosity. My awareness came when I heard a dead tree branch snap, but when I turned to look, no animal was to be seen. Trudging along, I continued to feel that I was being followed.

After a time, I stopped and turned, but didn't sight my follower. Some minutes later, instead of stopping, I just whipped around. Now I saw my tracker. A large black wolf that immediately darted into concealment.

I turned and continued snowshoeing, wondering why the wolf was following me. Then I remembered that I had not eaten one of the two meat sandwiches that I had prepared and packaged for my lunch. Could the wolf scent the meat that was wrapped in waxed paper and concealed in my canvas satchel? I believed it could. A while later, on arriving at the edge of my home clearing, I stopped, removed the satchel, unwrapped the sandwich, and placed it on the snow. Then I walked on. After taking about forty steps, I stopped and turned around.

The wolf had clearly eaten the meat from my sandwich. It was now sitting upright, mouth agape in a lupine smile, and staring at me in a neighborly manner.

Since that time, I have made friends with many wolves. Some twenty-five years ago, while sleeping out, I was honored when at first light the leader of one pack that I had been studying for several years urinated on the foot of my canvas-covered sleeping bag. As I looked up, he backed away a step, scratched several times with his hind feet, wagged his tail, and turned to rejoin his pack. Five other wolves had evidently been admiring their leader's daring, for they, too, stood smiling, tails wagging. When the leader joined them, they all ran off, gamboling like puppies and howl-barking at intervals.

Since my first lupine encounter I have learned a lot about wolves and as a result I consider them to be loyal, highly intelligent, and, finally, affectionate companions who are able to communicate their feelings in simple, but direct, ways. Of course, that early morning in northwestern Ontario I learned that wolves do not attack humans.

Would that men did not attack others of their kind — or any other creature that comes their way. The world would be a peaceful place if we humans all learned to behave like wolves.

7
Sharon's Foxes

On October, 24, 1994, my wife, Sharon, received a fax message from the Midland and District Humane Society of Ontario. The sender was Christine Mason, the wildlife co-ordinator. She needed someone to take care of an injured fox.

Because Sharon has, in recent years, successfully rehabilitated a number of individual foxes — all of which, when fully recovered, have been released on our well-treed, one-hundred-acre property — it has become known that my wife has developed a rapport with these high-strung wildlings. We were not surprised by the latest request. I faxed a return dictated by Sharon: "Yes! When?"

Four days later, Christine and the young vixen fox arrived. The animal was in a bad way. She had evidently been hit a slanting blow by a car as she was crossing a highway and the impact had tossed her onto the side of the road. The driver who caused the injury may or may not have been aware of the accident, but the fact is that the young fox was left lying on the gravel shoulder in a semi-conscious condition.

Fortunately for the vixen, however, the driver of an approaching car noticed the fox when the vehicle's headlights reflected on her white underparts. Even more fortuitously, the driver and his wife were compassionate people. They stopped the car, approached the fox, and, noting her condition, picked her up and in due course took her to a veterinarian. The fox's main injury was a long rip on the front of her left leg. The wound was an inch wide and reached from just below the knee to the joint (ankle) of her foot.

In the clinic, the vixen was injected with an antibiotic and an effort was made to suture the long injury, but it was too wide to close — the sutures broke through the edges of the skin.

Four days later, on September 14, after the couple who rescued her had paid an exorbitant veterinary fee, Zorra (Spanish for female fox), as we were to name her, was taken to the Midland and District Humane Society. There she was X-rayed: no broken bones. But the wound had to be thoroughly cleaned, for during the previous four days it had become seriously infected. Additionally, the Humane Society's veterinarian diagnosed severe radial nerve damage and noted that if regeneration were to occur, it would probably take at least four months.

Christine Mason and her assistant, Lori Kitchen, began to work on the fox. Daily she had to be given an antibiotic injection, after which the wound had to be cleaned and a new dressing applied to the leg. This task was difficult at first. Christine had to grab the fox by the scruff of the neck and hold her still while Lori applied a bandage around the muzzle, an impromptu control that prevented the frightened animal from biting her rescuers.

Day by day the infection responded to treatment. Zorra's appetite was good and soon it was no longer necessary to bandage the leg. But although there was no sign of regeneration, the skinless injury appeared as a long, dry, inch-wide red stripe that no longer showed signs of weeping or infection.

Christine brought Zorra to us on October 28, and once again the special part of our basement that had often served as a convalescent home for a number of other care-needing wild animals of different species was put into service.

Our basement "hospital ward" has a floor of earth cluttered here and there by large Cambrian granite rocks that are somewhat flattened on top. When we acquired the property a number of years ago, the previous owners had added a section to the house. They had intended to cement the new basement's floor, as they had done for the main basement, but the Cambrian granite made digging impossible below the five-foot level. So, afraid that mice and other creatures would tunnel below the footings and make their way into the house, they built a wall separating the earth part from the cement part. As a result, the "hospital ward" is ten feet wide by twenty-eight feet long, has a ceiling height of five feet, and a small, hinged and latched door that is covered by heavy wire mesh. For winter occupants, there is an electric heater suspended from one of the ceiling beams. And although a relatively small window has been installed at each end of the basement, an electric bulb, which is turned on when needed, is also suspended from the ceiling.

Apart from the relatively few occasions when I must enter the dungeon (as I think of it) to change the bulb, or to ensure that the latest temporary occupant has not dug out our water line, which, buried about eight inches below the earth, traverses the ten-foot width of the earthen sanctuary to enter the main basement, I keep myself on the sidelines. I am available if needed. And, as time passes, I am able to make contact to some degree with the inhabitants, but I generally leave the care giving to my very efficient rehabilitator.

Zorra arrived in mid-afternoon and was immediately released into the basement, where a dish of chicken and cooked meat awaited her beside the water container. That done, the fox was left alone for the rest of the day and through the night so that she could explore and become relatively comfortable in her new quarters after, and of necessity, having been confined in a small cage for forty-five days.

Next morning Sharon began the care routines that she has developed over the years. Morning, noon, and evening she entered Zorra's quarters and, with the patience of Job, talked to her, offered her special treats, and, quite literally, communed with her.

Now there are those who might think that attempting to

commune in silence with an animal is an impossibility. Not so. If a person has the patience, is fully relaxed, speaks quietly in greeting, and by his or her mien shows open affection, an animal will sooner or later respond and will become comfortable with that person. That is exactly how Sharon has gained the trust of all the animals that have so far come into her care. And that was how she gained Zorra's trust. Day after day she would go down to the basement, enter Zorra's quarters, and, after setting down special foods, she would sit quietly, communicating silently with her ward, willing the injury to heal.

One week after Zorra came to us, we found that she liked peanuts. This was not too surprising, for we have yet to find a mammal that does not like peanuts, strange as this may seem. The nuts are, in effect, alien food, but their odor and taste are always eagerly accepted. So I began to make a point of going to Zorra's doorway two or three times a day, opening the window and putting a few shelled peanuts on the inside ledge. At first, the fox ran away to hide behind a cedar shelter the moment that I approached the window, but after several days, she began to wait for me as soon as she heard me descending the basement steps, having soon been able to distinguish between the sounds of Sharon's footsteps and mine. At that time, she would take a position about four feet from the window and, although quite evidently prepared to run away if she thought that I was about to enter the basement, she would allow me to open the window and put half a dozen nuts on the sill. In the end, Zorra picked up courage and would come to me and take peanuts from my fingers. Which was something that she had started to do after only a few days with Sharon!

When Zorra first arrived, she walked mainly on three legs. Two weeks later, however, she started to put some weight on the injured limb, but she could only manage to balance the leg on the wrist, the paw being bent backwards, knuckles down against the ground. It was painful to watch her as she tried to use all four legs.

By the first week of December, however, she was trying hard to bring forward the toes of her injured foot; then on the 11th she was able to spread the toes and to actually walk with the toes extended. Now and then, when lifted clear of the ground, the toes were pulled backwards.

On December 23 Zorra started to walk on all four feet, albeit that she limped with the right leg. Nevertheless, she could now dig with both front paws. And the skin and fur had re-grown on her injured leg! The only sign now left of the dreadful injury was a red spot, the size of a dime, that persisted below the "elbow."

Despite the almost amazing progress she had made, Zorra was not ready for release until spring. On May 8, Sharon, doing her best to hold back tears, opened one of the convalescent room's windows and lifted Zorra, pushing her through to freedom.

We did not expect to see Zorra again; at least, not in daytime. But we always put out food at night in strategic areas of our property, so we were sure that Zorra would do well. And indeed she did!

As of this writing (October 15, 1995), Zorra comes to visit almost every night, and twice during the past week, while I was walking Freki — an old springer spaniel that Sharon rescued from almost certain death and brought home in our car — Zorra came along (following at a distance). She was not afraid of me and she certainly was not afraid of Freki, who is the most docile canine that I have ever known.

8
Adventure in Saskatchewan

In the summer of 1959, while exploring western Canada with my wolf-dog Yukon, a vibrant, 130-pound mischief maker, I stopped at a bison enclosure located south of Moose Jaw, Saskatchewan, a sanctuary established by the provincial government. A notice clipped to the fence advised the public to keep out of the large, fenced area. Although I was greatly interested in these plains buffalo, I generally respect such "keep-out" notices, not only because it is courteous to do so, but also because one just never knows what kind of law enforcers are to be met behind them.

Nevertheless, I was chagrined that not a single bison

showed its shaggy head and, although I was unusually patient for more than an hour, I finally decided that there were no buffalo behind the tall, page-wire fencing. Yukon, who scoffed at law and order, had been most impatient while I waited, sawing at the lead, which I held tightly, and whining quite pitifully. After my period of inactivity, and my companion's urge to romp over the bald prairie, which we had only just encountered after driving along an arrowstraight, paved highway to right and left of which was nothing but farms and cattle, I, too, hankered to explore the prairie.

So, egged on by Yukon, I began to walk beside the fence, seeking a spot through which I might be able to enter the sanctuary. I failed to find such a place, but Yukon, more adept at nefarious invasions, found one just as I was about to give up. It consisted of a relatively small hole in an area where some of the wire had become quite rusty. The aperture was just large enough for me to squeeze through, half-dragged by Yukon, who had swiftly ducked through the opening while still connected to me by his lead.

Once inside I brushed the prairie dust from my clothing, unfastened Yukon's lead, and then, at random, I began to walk toward a rolling rise about 150 yards away. Yukon dashed away, disappearing over the rise. I wasn't worried because he could always track me down no matter how far away he was.

When I reached the rise, I was delighted to discover a fairly large slough (an area of marshy ground) that was swarming with ducks, most of which were just taking off after having been rudely disturbed by Yukon. But, as ducks will do, they soon alighted on the far side of the marsh some two hundred feet away while Yukon, uninterested in birds, romped away, and disappeared over another height of land.

Thus far I had seen a variety of birds, the ducks, and about a million biting flies of one kind or another. But no bison. Had the sign advertising their presence been erected by some prankster? Or had it perhaps been forgotten after the bison had been moved from the area?

I was disappointed, for I had been looking forward to seeing, close at hand, a herd of the shaggy bovines about which I had read but, with the exception of a few moth-eaten specimens exhibited by a couple of zoos, had never really seen. Disgruntled, I whistled for Yukon, turned around, and started to walk toward the fence and the exit hole.

I suppose I dawdled some, for, in truth, I was interested in the ducks and in the many different species of birds that graced the environment. In any event, I paid scant attention to my rear, knowing that when Yukon had had enough, he would come charging back to me. In fact, I was so engrossed by the birds, that I at first failed to hear a strange, rumbling noise that seemed to be rising behind me. Moments later the sound increased intensity and I stopped and looked back. But nothing was to be seen, so I continued walking toward the fence.

Suddenly, Yukon came rushing by me at full speed and although I called to him, he kept on running. Then the strange sound became loud. I turned. At an estimated distance of seventy-five yards a herd of about twenty bison were charging toward me, throwing up clouds of dust and bellowing as though demented!

I ran. I mean, I flew! I had no idea I could run so fast. With frantically beating heart I raced for the now seemingly distant fence while expecting at any moment to be trampled into a pulp by the ferocious beasts that were gaining upon me at a speed that I could not possibly match.

Then the fence loomed up. And the blessed hole. And Yukon, sitting happily on his haunches, *outside* the fence, and panting with pleasure, as though telling me: "Hey, skin one of those. I brought them for you, after all."

Well, because I am now writing about this stunt, it is obvious that I got out of that enclosure with a more or less whole skin, reaching the hole in time to dive through it while I was about a dozen feet ahead of the galloping herd.

My minor injuries resulted from my hasty slide through broken wire, but I held them to no account as I watched the buffalo stop, snort loudly, and stamp their front hooves, raising up a small cloud of prairie dust.

Why were the bison so aggressive, I asked myself? It was not until the next day that I learned from a government biologist that the cows had calves and were inclined to resent intrusion. That last comment was unnecessary. I knew that they had resented intrusion.

For a time I felt like throttling Yukon. But two mornings later, while camping in Saskatchewan's Cypress Hills — a fascinating region — I fully forgave Yukon when, as we were having our breakfast, we were scolded by a young, rather nasty-tempered park ranger who informed me loudly and angrily that dogs were not allow to run free in the park. Yukon was not running, as I pointed out to the young man, he was sitting beside me, quietly and peacefully.

"Well, you've got to put him on a lead or I'll charge you with a misdemeanor."

As the officious official was speaking, Yukon rose, wagged his tail, strode to the young man, and peed on his leg. The ranger was so intimidated by the huge dog that he just stood there, looking down as Yukon soaked his left pant leg and boot. When finished, Yukon stood back, stared at the ranger, scratched some dirt with his back feet, and trotted back to me, where he sat down.

As matters turned out, the ranger was not too bad a sort. He forgave Yukon, and he forgave me for laughing until my sides hurt. Then he joined us for breakfast.

9
A Shriek in the Forest Night

In *The Birds of Canada*, published by the National Museum (1966), W. Earl Godfrey notes that the call of the great horned owl consists of a "series of deep hoo notes, often five, which are less varied and deeper than the Barred Owl's; also a scream."

How true! But Dr. Godfrey's succinct comment cannot possibly describe the quality of the banshee-like wail that the owl suddenly launches in a darkened forest.

Imagine yourself in the deep woods at the midnight hour observing a small clearing with a young companion. The clearing has been baited with over-ripe fish in the hope of attracting a black bear so that the youngster may see one of these interesting mammals up close and, if possible, get a photograph of it.

The young fellow is the son of a friend. He is passionately interested in nature, but he has had little opportunity as yet to enter the night-time forest and observe its events firsthand.

The father asks me to take junior for a night trip; son pleads; mother reluctantly gives her consent; and I eventually accept responsibility for the tyro.

At 11 p.m. Peter and I set out from my property carrying camera, flashlight, thermos of coffee, and sandwiches. It was a Saturday in mid-July; the mosquitoes were kept more or less at bay with repellent. The full moon was just peeping above the tree line, a green-yellow lamp that promised to reveal itself fully, but was now and then dimmed by some slow-moving clouds — the fat, white kind that sail like stately galleons running before a favoring breeze.

The forest echoed with the voices of crickets, bullfrogs, and whippoorwills, the cries of nighthawks, and, occasionally, with the dry, crackling sounds made by the passage of small mammals, perhaps raccoons or porcupines.

We walked cautiously because I did not want to use a flash-light. And we talked quietly.

"Now, when we get to the bait areas," I instructed, "absolutely no talking. And you must keep still. If that bear hears us, he'll take off and we will have wasted the night."

"O.K.," said Peter.

Was he a little nervous, I wondered? Then I chuckled

quietly, patting his shoulder reassuringly. He spoke again.

"Why can't we use a flashlight?"

"If we use a flashlight, switching it on and off will alert the animals. Also, our eyes won't get used to the darkness. It's better in the forest night to walk slowly and let your feet 'see' for you. They will, you know. I can't explain this too well — you must sense it for yourself to understand it — but one sort of feels one's way with the feet. Once you get the hang of it, you'll find it's quite easy and, after a while, your eyes will get used to the night and will pick out objects that are in your way."

We were almost at the clearing now. I stopped, holding the lad's arm.

"O.K.," I instructed. "From now on, we speak in whispers and only when necessary. If the bear doesn't come within a couple of hours, we'll head back. Unless you'd like to stay all night?"

"No! A couple of hours'll be fine." He paused, then: "In a way, I kinda hope he doesn't come!"

So I explained that I had been feeding the bear since early spring and that if we just sat quietly and let him eat, then take his picture before he turns to leave, he would simply disappear in the bush.

I sensed that the young fellow was reassured. We walked farther and found a place in the lee of some large boulders — about thirty feet away from the ripe fish, the odor of which assailed us. Peter muttered softly: "Boy! It sure reeks!" After that, we settled down, remaining silent.

Presently, the moon rose above the trees, casting bizarre shadows on the grassy opening. The forest seemed to come alive with silver light and slow-moving shadows. The sounds of night were all around us.

We noticed the arrival of the great horned owl only because the big bird slipped as it landed on one of the branches of a nearby poplar; otherwise we would not have detected its presence. Like all owls, the margins of its feathers are softened, causing its flight to be almost totally silent.

I whispered these things to my companion, and warned him that the big owl would almost certainly call. We waited.

Minutes later, the owl's deep notes spilled out into the night and its sonorous echoes seemed to answer back. The young man listened, fascinated. But I paid scant attention to him, for I was watching the place where the game trail emptied into the clearing, the opening in which the bear would first appear, walking quietly on his fleshy pads.

Presently I saw a shadow darker than the rest; a moving shadow that stopped suddenly at the mouth of the trail. I was about to nudge my companion to alert him to the bear's presence, when the owl cut loose with its scream.

"Ohmigod!"

The young man's exclamation was so loud and high-pitched, his start so violent that the thermos and flashlight were dislodged from their places on the rock. The bear, as startled by the racket as the young man had been by the scream of the owl, whoofed loudly, wheeled deftly like a cavalry charger, and disappeared into the night, the sound of his going reaching us as a series of crashes. The wilderness became quiet after the bruin's abrupt departure.

My companion clutched my arm and I tried to tell him that it was only the owl that had caused the commotion, but laughter welled out of me instead, which was probably the best cure for the young fellow's frazzled nerves.

We retrieved the fallen items. The flashlight was broken, but the thermos was intact, and, since the vigil was now ended (for I knew that the bear would not return for many hours) we drank coffee and I explained about the owl's dreadful scream.

"It's intended to startle, you see; to make a hare, or a groundhog jump, revealing itself within the shadows to the owl's big, keen eyes.

"The smaller prey animals often become completely immobile if they feel that danger lurks in their surroundings, so they freeze and blend into the background. Then the owl is not sure of what they are. The bird can certainly see the indistinct shape, for they have great sight, but such an immobile object could be the head of a wolf, or a crouching fox, or even a tree stump. So, when it's not sure, the great horned owl yells suddenly and watches for reaction.

"If the object remains immobile, it is almost certainly a stump, or a rock. If it happens to be a resting wolf, coyote, or fox, it will be startled and reveal itself, and if it is a hare or a groundhog, it will also become startled. Such an animal may then run or it may jump. In either event, the owl will identify it and stoop for the kill."

An afterthought occurred to me.

"It's just as well that your mother wasn't here, or she'd be having a fit about now."

"And just what do you think that I'm having?"

The youngster's reply was serious enough, but it carried an underlying sense of humor. We retraced our journey home and I told him more about owls.

10
The Jailbird

A police cell would seem an odd place to find a snowy owl, but that is precisely where I took charge of Nyctea (as I was to name her). She had been "arrested" in the town of Whitby, Ontario, way back in the mid-1960s, for committing what may be described as two counts of common assault.

Nyctea's crimes? She had evidently injured her right wing by flying against a telephone wire and had thereafter landed in a backyard in which lived a dachshund, an inquisitive young dog who was undoubtedly of the opinion that anything that fell out of the sky and landed in his domain was his by right of tenure.

The dachshund, let it be said, was not at all aggressive. But, full of zest, he dashed up to the owl and, while bowing like the gentleman he was, thrust an inquisitive nose toward the bird, wagging his tail as though to say: "Hello, bird, let's play."

Alas, Nyctea was not in a playful mood. Her wing hurt, she was squatting on grass instead of being perched some distance above the ground, and she had never before met a creature that seemed to propel itself forward on legs that were obviously too short for the bulk of its owner. When the dog's shiny black nose approached Nyctea, the owl fluffed up her feathers, spread her good wing, and pecked the dachshund's proboscis. The dog, more astonished than hurt, began to yap and run around the owl, trying to approach it, but always held at bay by the now furious snowy. The commotion alerted the dachshund's owner, a stout gentleman who took the dog into the house and then called the police, claiming that the bird had seriously injured the dog. He requested that *someone* remove the offending creature from his yard.

In due course a very large policeman arrived. He entered the garden, stooped over the owl — who fixed its baleful eyes on the man in blue — and reached downward with his hands spread. Nyctea fluffed her feathers, spread one wing, and when a hand came into range, lunged forward and struck with one foot, a single sharp talon scratching the officer's index finger, causing it to bleed.

The constable, however, was made of stern stuff. Sucking the injured finger, he knocked at the house door. When it was opened by the stout owner, he asked the man if he could have a bandage. One was produced. Now, with his blood staunched, the officer asked for a sack. None was available. But an old bath towel could be had.

The minion of the law accepted the offering, returned to the garden, stopped just out of beak and claw range, and spread the towel over the bird. Nyctea was captured. But how does one drive a police cruiser while holding a large and struggling owl with one hand? One does not. The constable radioed his headquarters and a second cruiser was dispatched, one whose driver had loaded in his car a large cardboard box.

Nyctea was ignominiously thrust into the box and carted off to the hoosegow, where she was locked up as a malefactor. She quickly thrust her way out of the box, managing afterward to perch on the back of a chair. The question then was: "What do we do with an owl in our jail?"

Somebody suggested that I be contacted. The suggestion was unanimously agreed upon and, two hours after the owl had been incarcerated, I arrived in my station wagon, in which I had loaded a large avian cage.

The arresting officer, looking very sheepish, led me to Nyctea's cell, opened the door, and suggested that I enter with my cage and capture her. While I slowly approached the prisoner so as not to startle her, the large constable stayed outside, well clear of the cell door.

As it happened, Nyctea, still perched on the back of the wooden chair, was easy to capture. I asked the officer to wave his hand suddenly and, as I expected, the owl locked her gaze upon her erstwhile victim, allowing me to catch her from the rear with both hands, holding her wings in place and keeping clear of her curved talons. Moments later she was housed in the cage.

When I returned to my property, I put Nyctea in a large cage that contained several roosting bars and fed her with strips of chicken, a supply of which I had bought on my way home. Each strip of white meat was first dunked in water, for I felt sure that the bird was dehydrated. The first piece was taken suspiciously, body feathers fluffed up, one wing stretched out, but as soon as she had tasted the food, she accepted five more strips without showing signs of aggression.

By now I knew that her left wing had been injured in some way and I was concerned, for the bones of birds are hollow and heal very badly, often needing to be pinned. How could I examine the owl?

After some debate, I determined that there was only one way. Experience in caring for wild mammals and birds has taught me to have on hand a variety of items that are useful for controlling injured strays. Among these are several hoods of various sizes that I have made for subduing birds of prey prior to examination. The little "hat" is fastened around the neck with strips of gauze bandage. In addition, I have a supply of bandages, which I use for various purposes. With birds, especially owls and hawks, I use the bandages to secure their legs with the soft ties.

When Nyctea was immobilized after something of a struggle during which she thrust one talon through the first knuckle of my left thumb, I examined her wing. Although it was quite seriously bruised, I was relieved to find that it was not broken.

In due course, Nyctea got to know me and allowed me to handle her when this was necessary. She remained in my care for that entire summer.

Snowy owls are denizens of the north, usually inhabiting a huge, circumpolar range along the Arctic tundras. In North America they range from northern Labrador to northern Alaska, south to Hudson's Bay, and north to Ellesmere Island.

Unlike most owls, snowies hunt by day as well as by night, a necessity for a bird that lives in a region where the midnight sun burns late in summer and disappears entirely during winter.

Sometimes, when the lemming population in their range has dropped due to competition for food and space, the snowies head south and may be seen as far from their range as the middle states in the United States.

Males are mainly white, but females, like Nyctea, have a profusion of brownish bars decorating their white feathers. Females, whose wings each measure about sixteen inches, are larger than males, measuring about twenty-seven inches in the body as opposed to about twenty-four inches for the males.

In September I set Nyctea free, expecting her to soar away, never to be seen again. I was wrong. She stayed in my region until the snows piled quite high, then, one morning, she landed near my front door, sat on a log, and looked at me. I like to think that she was thanking me before saying good-bye.

She spread her wings, waited just long enough for me to photograph her, and then rose, heading northward. I was not to see her again.

11
The Hummingbird and the Burdock

One morning in mid-June, while I was strolling across an open area in which grew bushes and wildflowers, I was attracted by movement on top of a burdock bur. Curious, I walked toward the plant, but before I had covered half the distance I was able to determine the cause of the movement: a ruby-throated hummingbird female. The tiny bird had gotten herself hopelessly tangled among the hooked bracts above which grow lavender-colored little flowers, the presence of which had obviously attracted the bird.

The bird, a mature female — her sex immediately obvious by the absence of the ruby flashes that characterize the male's throat feathers — was fighting the bur, but the more she struggled, the more she became entangled.

Approaching slowly, I soon realized that I would not be able to free the hummer with just my fingers. So with my right hand, I used my penknife to slowly cut through the plant's stem, while with my left hand I gently held the bird and her imprisoning bur.

The moment I turned away from the burdock, the entangled bird became passive. This worried me. Was she going into stress? Holding the tiny captive in the palm of my left hand, my fingers loosely curled around her, I hurried to my cabin. Inside, I picked up a pair of sharp-pointed surgical scissors and a pair of tweezers. Next, because there was not enough light to work by within the building, I went outside, settled myself on a nearby boulder, and, continuing to hold bird and bur in my open palm, began to snip off the hooks and to pull them away gently with the tweezers.

The task was laborious; each time I cut a hook from the bur I had to put down the scissors and pick up the tweezers, then, very slowly and gently, remove an individual hook and set it aside. Her eyes followed my every movement, and the intelligence that shone from each of her pupils convinced me that, far from being stressed, she was aware that I was helping her.

Right on the heels of that thought I questioned myself. Was I exaggerating? Was it likely that a tiny creature with a brain that was smaller than a dried pea could possibly know my intention? Was I being anthropomorphic and ascribing human attributes to a nonhuman entity?

As my tiny "patient" continued to remain docile, I began to

feel that she was, in fact, aware that she was being helped and, furthermore, that she instinctively knew it was in her best interests to cooperate by remaining still.

Throughout the time that I worked on her, she kept her body still. And when the last of the vicious hooks was removed, she continued for some seconds to remain quiet in my open hand; then she stood up, shook her feathers in place, hopped to the end of my fingers, shook again, and turned her head to look at me. Then she flew away. I had timed the process. It had taken me thirty-five minutes to remove all the burs.

Watching as she flew toward a solitary hawthorn that stood about nine feet tall, I could hardly bring myself to credit that the bird had accepted my help so calmly, even to the point of tidying her feathers while sitting on my hand! I continued to watch her progress and very soon after she had left me, she reached the hawthorn and disappeared within its thorny embrace. Her anxiety to reach the hawthorn suggested that she almost certainly had young!

Hawthorns, *Crataegus* species (there are more than one thousand different species of hawthorns, between twenty and thirty of which are found in various locations across Canada), belong to a group of very dense shrubs or small trees, the branches and main trunks of which are dressed with leaves as well as with long, shiny, and sharp-pointed thorns, some of them reaching a length of two inches.

Because hummingbird females are too small to defend their eggs or chicks from the raids of birds such as shrikes, starlings, and grackles, they nest in trees or shrubs where their tiny nests and minute young are completely hidden and hard to get at. I felt sure that the bird I had rescued was either building her nest, or had already done so and had laid two tiny eggs in it, or had already hatched her chicks. That was why she had flown directly to the hawthorn.

Although I was eager to peek into the tree so as to see the nest and the eggs or the chicks, I controlled the urge. Instead, I sat down on the young grasses of the clearing and kept watch on the hawthorn. Only three minutes after I had taken up my position, the hummingbird flew out of the tree and raced over my head with wings that were beating so rapidly that they could not be individually distinguished.

The bird's quick exit from the hawthorn suggested that she had young: after she had been freed she had clearly flown to her nest to ensure that the chicks were safe; then she had emerged to seek food for them. When she disappeared I walked to her tree and peered into it. In a nest that was about the size and shape of a walnut were two chicks. I did not disturb them, but I was able to see that they were relatively newly hatched. They had not yet opened their eyes — an event that takes place about one week after hatching — and were each slightly larger than a honey bee and almost entirely naked, exposing their slate-blue skin.

Looking at the tiny beings I remembered that I had last year examined an abandoned nest containing an addled egg. That nest was beautiful. And having previously examined two others (after the young had been born and had left their tiny sanctuary), I knew that each little cup is designed so that it sits point down astride a thin branch. The inside walls of the cups are fashioned from a mix of bud scales — the tiny leaves of undeveloped shoots — and the down of plants such as thistles and dandelions. The outsides of the nests are covered by bits of lichen and moss and are held together by spider silks.

Just after dawn the morning after I had helped the hummingbird, I stationed myself on a relatively open spot, my back against a medium-size red maple, and waited for the bird to emerge from her nest. My location was about one hundred feet away from her nesting tree. I planned to log every one of her foraging and feeding trips.

Before the sun had properly cleared the eastern tree line, the bird emerged from the hawthorn. She came out so swiftly that I almost missed her, but I did manage to catch a glimpse as she flew overhead. She seemed to be aiming for the area where she had gotten caught by the burdock, but, I was glad to see, she steered clear of the spikey plants and soon disappeared in an area of sparse young maple trees beneath which grew trilliums and white clintonias. I started to time her as soon as I saw her. From the time she flew over me to the time she returned and entered her nest, seven minutes had elapsed. As soon as she disappeared in the hawthorn, I reset the stopwatch. She spent three minutes with her chicks.

I remained on station for five hours. During that time, pausing only for short rests inside her nest tree, the tiny bird made forty-three trips in search of food. How such a tiny being could nourish itself during the frequent journeying and at the same time suck up nectar or catch minute spiders with which to feed her young seemed to me almost miraculous.

Flying up, down, straight ahead, and backward, humming-birds are remarkable gymnasts. The tiny ruby-throat

(*Archilochus colubris*) and its kin migrate north during the spring, a journey from Mexico to Canada!

It has been said that these little flyers cross the Gulf of Mexico during their migrations north and south. I cannot accept that. The birds would have to fly nonstop for six hundred miles! What I suspect is that they coast around the shoreline and when fatigued they stop to rest and feed.

Whoever named the ruby-throated hummingbird had little regard for the females of the species, since only the male has a ruby throat. Perhaps the name emerged when it was noted that the males of the species have but a very brief courtship with the females and then leave their spouses to raise their young without assistance. (Usually a female hummingbird incubates her eggs for sixteen days. When the tiny fledglings emerge, she feeds the ravenous chicks for about nineteen days, when most nestlings leave the nest.) Not only that, but once the mating time is over, the humming Lotharios actually chase away their erstwhile mates from sources of nectar!

Nevertheless, the little females do not appear to need the assistance of their chauvinistic partners, for the energy expended by female hummers during only one hour of foraging would probably leave their mates gasping for breath!

Whether male or female, however, when a ruby-throat is hovering, it uses about the same amount of energy as a human running at a speed of about ten miles an hour. For this reason, these tiny fliers must feed every ten or fifteen minutes. If a bird has not eaten enough by late evening, it would die of starvation were it not for the fact that under such conditions it is able to put itself into a state of torpor. Its metabolism slows right down and stays that way until morning, when it recovers instantly and flies away to drink nectar, which it does between sixty and seventy times during daylight hours, sipping honeydew from the flowers. It also eats tiny insects, such as aphids and small spiders.

The female that I rescued from the burdock seemed to accept my presence near her while she was hovering at a flower and so I was able to observe some aspects of her metabolism. Watching her as she hovered over a flower while sipping nectar through her extensile, hollow tongue fascinated me. From early studies, I knew that her wings were beating at a rate of between fifty and sixty times a *second*. But I had not hitherto been close enough to a feeding humming-bird to note the rate of its heart. This time I was privileged to watch the cardiac rhythm, but I was quite unable to time it — it was much too fast! I was amazed to note that the tiny body shook constantly in response to the heart beats. And then, when it had emptied the nectar supply from the bloom, it suddenly darted away, attaining a speed that I knew had been clocked at between thirty and thirty-five miles per hour!

Knowing that ruby-throated hummingbird young emerge from the egg between eighteen and twenty days after the start of incubation, I kept an eye on the nesting area, not going too close for fear of disturbing the mother. Approximately nineteen days after the mother had laid her eggs, one of her young, a male, alighted on the roof of my car during mid-afternoon.

I was outside at the time and only about three yards from the vehicle, so I was fortunate enough to see him as he landed. Not wishing to disturb the tiny bird, however, I kept my distance, but a moment later I noted that the ruby-throat was struggling on the car's shiny roof.

I approached the vehicle, expecting that my presence would give the youngster enough energy to launch itself into space. But he ignored me and continued to struggle. That was when I realized the cause of the bird's predicament: squatting on his short legs, every time he flapped his wings to create a launch, the ends of the feathers hit the car's roof and prevented lift-off.

I walked to the car, noting as I arrived that the bird had become quiet. I lifted my arm, held my hand open, and slowly moved it up to the bird. Without hesitation he climbed on my index finger. There, so securely perched that I could feel his little claws grasping my flesh, he shuffled his feathers. That done, he put them all back in place. Next, turning his tiny head to look at me, he chirped and launched himself away, flying well and soon disappearing from sight.

Nature taught me one more lesson that morning: The roofs of automobiles and other slippery or flat surfaces are bad landing places for tiny, short-legged birds that have been designed to launch away from branches, or upright tree trunks. More important, however, was the awareness that such a small being could understand that I was not his enemy, that I was, in fact, his rescuer.

12

Do Animals Think?

If you ask a number of people at the same time whether animals think, you are likely to receive at least six different answers.

Those who believe that humans have dominion over the "lower animals" will most probably say "no." But those individuals who have experienced the love and companionship of such domestic pets as horses, dogs, and cats will likely say "yes," although some of them may seek to qualify their answers by adding something like: "well, dogs and cats and horses can think, but I don't know about wild animals." Others, openly uncaring, may say that they do not know because they have not given the matter any thought.

Behavioral psychologists, on the other hand, will certainly hedge their answers. Some, like the writer of a behavior text book published in 1981, might say: "Animals can be goal-directed without being purposeful, and they can behave appropriately without knowing why."

This observation is applied to all animals, domestic or wild, and is a view that seems to be shared by those who conduct animal experimentation — who treat the sentient beings upon whom they inflict pain "in the cause of science," or "in the cause of beauty aids," as though they can neither reason, nor suffer.

Some behaviorists go further, however. In *Behaviorism, Science and Human Nature* (New York: Norton, 1982), B. Schwartz and H. Lacey noted: "If you want to know why someone did something, do not ask. Analyze the person's immediate environment until you find the reward [for the action]. If you want to change someone's actions, do not reason or persuade. Find the reward and eliminate it. The idea that people are autonomous and possess within them the power and the reason for making decisions *has no place in behavior theory.*" (my italics)

The above quote would have us believe that if Schwartz and Lacey are right and humans cannot make conscious decisions, then animals cannot do so either!

The sixth answer will be "Yes! Animals can and do think." That, most certainly, would be my own reply.

Some years ago, at a time when I was writing a syndicated nature column, I came across a report by a behaviorist who had tested a number of animals in his laboratory in order to determine which of the species was gifted with the highest intelligence. Most of the animals were domestic, such as horses and dogs. But the scientist also tested a beaver, which, he later decided, was five times less intelligent than a dog.

When I finished reading the report, I was intensely annoyed, not only because I had encountered yet another example of convoluted, psycho-babble thinking, but also because years earlier I had concluded that IQ testing of animals (or peoples for that matter) produced invalid results. In addition, it seemed to me to be utterly ridiculous that a psychologist should take into his laboratory a totally wild animal and expect it to perform on par with domestic animals (that for thousands of years have been accustomed to the world of humans) a series of tricks conducted in a sterile and alien environment.

That week I wrote a column on the subject, first explaining that my rebuttal did not in any way belittle the intelligence of dogs, then deriding the methods employed to test the beaver's intellect. Finally, I noted that until the psychologist could show me a dog that was capable of constructing a beaver dam, I would continue to argue against his findings, just as I would argue against anyone who might suggest that a beaver could chase a ball, or could retrieve a ball.

My column was published Canada-wide. Not long after that particular piece got into print, I received an invitation to speak to a group of behavioral psychologists during one of their meetings. I agreed, although I knew full well that the invite had teeth in it: during the usual question period, the psychologists wanted to chastise me for daring to criticize their science.

And it was so, although at first I was able to answer a great many easy and expected questions in a satisfactory way while remaining on guard for the one that would come sooner or later. Fifteen minutes into the question period, it came.

"You contend that IQ testing is valueless and have derided it publicly. Can you, therefore, define for us your idea of intelligence?"

The speaker was quite obviously annoyed with me.

"Intelligence, I believe, is demonstrated by those organisms that are capable of living successfully within their own environments. By that measure, all of us in this room, and, indeed, most members of the human species, have failed, for it can hardly be claimed that we are now living success-fully in our world," I replied.

To my surprise, that answer received considerable applause from my hostile audience. But afterward, when we went on to discuss animal thinking, nothing I could say was able to persuade the gathering that animals can think for themselves.

Instead, every speaker insisted that animals are entirely governed by genetic programming that came into being millions of years ago. In this, the psychologists were correct, but only partly so.

There is no doubt that genes, those sub-microscopic carriers of ancestral instructions, were "programmed" eons ago in all living things. Now, the science of genetics is too complex to explain fully here, but if we use computer terms, the invisible messengers from long ago will be recognized as being similar to the basic chips that allow a computer user to start up the system and to feed into its specific software programs.

Just as a computer user has at his or her disposal all the necessary equipment and power to use the machine and to write nature articles or letters, or tote up the bank balance, so are living entities genetically equipped with "basic programs" that allow them to enter the world equipped emotionally and rationally and able to function according to the demands and needs of their particular species. It is no accident that all mammals and many other vertebrates are furnished with sophisticated central nervous systems that include the brain — which is variously divided but which, for simplicity here, can be classed as the cerebrum (cortex) and the middle brain.

The brain, and through it the entire central nervous system, is partly influenced by the hereditary codes implanted in the genes, and partly by environmental events. If an animal is going to do the job right and survive for the term of its appointed life span, it must, like the computer user, combine its hardware (the genes) with its software (the brain), especially the cortex, which is the thinking part of the system that can quickly interpret environmental stimuli and decide just as quickly the appropriate responses to them.

Environmental signals reach an organism through its eyes, ears, nose, taste, hair, and the bottoms of its feet. Being adept at picking up signals is good, but it would be a useless exercise if the animal was unable to use its mind to determine the advantages or disadvantages of the signals.

Those animals that have complex nervous systems must exercise their memory powers, for they receive, and must catalog, literally thousands of environmental signals. The majority of these signals will be encountered for the first time at a very early age. In other words, they must *learn*, just like humans must begin to learn, soon after birth. In order to learn, animals must be capable of thought. Then too, if they are to be successful, they must be able to improvise, and to rationalize, or else they will not be able to deal successfully with the challenges of their environment. They are, it is true, helped by their genetic heritage, but they are nevertheless gifted with the power to make conscious decisions. When one sees, as I have done, the many ways in which animals give proof of their rationalness, there can be no doubt about the fact that they can think.

Recently, my wife and I watched a captive female wolf figure out a way in which to get a rope that was outside her enclosure. When she could not reach the target by sticking a paw through the wire and raking the rope toward her, she stood back, pondered, then tried lying flat on her side so as to push her muzzle through the two-by-four-inch mesh. She failed again. But then, still in the same position, she managed to open her mouth slightly and she stuck out her tongue, stretching it to its fullest. The tongue contacted the rope. The wolf then slid the tip of her tongue under the target and flipped it toward her. She did this three times, until the rope was near enough for her to grab it with her mouth!

It is said that thought is not possible without language and here, again, we are given an example of the arrogance of humanism and, especially, of the single-minded approach taken by some behavior specialists.

True, animals do not communicate in any kind of structured, human-like language, but they can "speak," and they are adept at body language, an art that humans have lost for the most part. Wolves, whales, dolphins, fish, monkeys, hyenas, chipmunks, squirrels, birds, etc., etc., all vocalize and have specific whistles, barks, growls, or other sounds that they employ for specific needs. We may not understand what a dolphin or a wolf is telling a companion, just as we are not likely to understand a Kalahari Bushperson unless we know his or her very difficult language. But does this mean that because we cannot understand certain kinds of vocal expressions, they should not be classed as language? Obviously not!

I give the last word on this subject to Dr. Donald R. Griffin, a professor at the Rockefeller University, who, in *Animal Thinking* (Harvard University Press, 1984), says: "The behaviorist viewpoint has been accepted, implicitly if not explicitly, by most ethologists studying animal behavior, so it is not surprising that they learn very little about animal thoughts and feelings."

13
Matilda

Matilda was a skunk. Like all of her kind, the basic black of her glossy coat was decorated with the characteristic white stripes that ran from the base of her bushy tail and along her flanks to join together at the back of her head, then continued as one thin line to the tip of her shiny, inquisitive nose.

Matilda and I met twenty-five years ago at two o'clock one summer morning while I was camping alone in the Ontario backwoods on the shores of a wilderness lake. In those days the water was clear and clean, and I could drink it without fear of being poisoned by industrial fallout and agricultural spray.

I almost shot Matilda with the anesthetic dart gun I carried for research purposes, but I refrained because the strength of the drug was intended for black bears, which I was studying at the time, and would have killed her. Also, because she was too close to me, had I murdered her, she would have repaid me before she died by stinking out my person, my tent, and my entire campsite with the potent liquid with which these pretty little animals defend themselves.

As it was, on first acquaintance, since she was actually crawling into my shelter, squeezing under the zipper, all I could think of doing for my protection was to squirt her with the small, hand-sprayer (aerosol sprays are not part of my outdoor equipment) that was filled with insect repellent.

I had earlier switched on my flashlight, disturbed by the skunk's scratching — the beam did not dismay my visitor — so I picked up the sprayer and pumped the handle several times. Matilda sneezed, wiped a front paw over her nose, and looked amazed. She was no doubt astounded that the creature whose lair she was invading was capable of spraying in self-defense with a liquid that, if not as lasting or evil smelling as her own, was at least unpleasant and irritating.

At any rate, her head and shoulders were quickly withdrawn from my tent and I was able to crawl out of my sleeping bag with some semblance of dignity instead of leaving the tent by cutting my way through one of its walls, as I would almost certainly have done had she succeeded in entering through the door. I cautiously exited through the doorway, raising the zipper slowly so as to make the least possible amount of noise.

Stepping outside, I was surprised to see Matilda. I had believed that having been shown by the tent's occupant that she was not welcome at the camp, Matilda would have taken the hint and departed. But she obviously had no intention of doing anything of the kind. Foolishly, I had neglected to wash the pan in which I had fried my supper bacon and Matilda had found this by the time I emerged from the tent. When my light located her she was busy lapping up the fat from the pan and although I stamped my feet and pretended to advance toward her in what I hoped was a threatening manner, she ignored me.

Now, realizing that I was being given an opportunity to study at close quarters a wild skunk who had probably never been in contact with humans before this, I decided to watch her. To do so with clarity, but also in the hope that she might leave if more light was available, I primed my gasoline lantern and lit it. When the strong white light flooded the campsite Matilda looked up at me and, I am sure, actually showed approval. Now she could see clearly, and since she had just then lapped up the last of the bacon fat, she left the pan and started looking around for other discarded items. Then she began to walk directly to me.

Discretion urged me to retreat and let Matilda have the campsite, but I was now intrigued by her — and curious to see what she would do if I remained still and allowed her the freedom of the camp. Since I was clad only in shorts, I reasoned that if the worst happened and I was sprayed, the job of cleaning myself would not be too great. So, nervously, I held my ground.

Matilda came right up to me and sniffed inquisitively at my

bare feet from a distance of about three inches; whether belonging to human or any other mammal, the soles of the feet and hands (front paws) are equipped with more scent glands than any other part of the body. As the skunk smelled me, I smelled her. She was emitting a faint trace of musk, a not unpleasant taint in that strength.

Evidently satisfied that I was neutral and thus harmless, she went around me and continued looking for food. I tried moving slowly. She did not so much as glance at me. I became brave. I had food in my pack, which was suspended from a tree some thirty feet from the tent. I lowered the supplies, opened the pack, and took some bread from it. When I returned to the tent area, the skunk turned to look at me, her nose twitching, no doubt at the scent of the bread. I threw her a piece. She pounced on it and ate it swiftly. I gave her more, throwing each piece closer to myself. In the next fifteen minutes she ate three entire slices, the last being consumed within a yard of my feet. Afterward, I went to bed, leaving Matilda in possession of the campsite.

The next day was Saturday and the lonely lake received visitors who, to me at least, were unwelcome. A party of fishermen arrived in an evil-smelling motorboat. The four men landed complete with beer and much noise.

Such an invasion I had not expected in a location that was more than one hundred miles from the nearest urban area. I was not outwardly hostile, but I was definitely aloof. Indeed, I decided that I would move out by canoe the next morning and head to my second research station, a distance of fifteen miles. Fortunately, the group went fishing as soon as a small tent had been put up, so the noise they made during the course of the day was at least weakened by distance. But that evening and on until one o'clock, the foursome regaled me with smutty jokes, with loud guffaws, and with arguments about baseball and hockey, subjects about which I know nothing and care less. At last, mercifully, the gang went to sleep, one man doing so outside in a sleeping bag, as the tent was too small to accommodate them all.

Some two hours later I was awakened by a crescendo of ear-splitting yells. The manly racket came from nearby. In fact, from my unwelcome neighbors. It was caused by Matilda, bless her!

Later I learned the sequence of events. Evidently Matilda had found the man sleeping outdoors and had decided that his chest would be an ideal place on which to rest awhile. Matilda, I estimated, weighed about four pounds — average for an adult female skunk — and her weight on his body awakened the sleeper. Since the moon was full, the startled oaf raised his head to peer into Matilda's beady eyes. She, curious lady, stretched forward the better to see the face, whereupon the man exploded into back-arching action, flinging Matilda into the air as he did so.

Matilda objected to such treatment. When she landed, she was already in position to fire her salvo, her body bent in a U: that is, her head and her business end both aiming at the threshing figure. She fired. Two thin streams of yellow, sticky fluid emerged with force, collided about twelve inches from the shooting glands, and formed a dense, choking, eye-stinging spray that enveloped the man, his sleeping bag, and the nearby tent.

At this point, the victim's companions emerged hurriedly from their tent, each brandishing a rifle which he was unable to use, for Matilda fired two more streams of her powerful juice. It was a rout! Immediately afterward, a sedate Matilda walked away, bushy tail held high and all four men ran to the lake and, cold as the water was, they dove in. But their efforts were of no avail. Matilda had done her work well, and I was grateful to her, for the quartet packed up and left the area by first light.

The next night Matilda came to visit me anew, but this time she came accompanied by three miniature skunklets that followed wherever she led. I spent an hour feeding the family and studying their behavior. For another five nights Matilda brought her young to visit with me, then I had to move to my other station.

Matilda taught me a great deal about the skunk, which is one of the maligned denizens of the wilderness. Whisper "skunk" in the hearing of the average urbanite and one is suddenly left alone. But there is really no reason to fear skunks provided one is careful to move slowly and calmly and to speak softly when in proximity of one of these friendly animals. When one makes their acquaintance in these ways, one finds that skunks are pleasant, interesting, and gentle beings. And they play an important role in the wilderness by eating many insects and cleaning up carrion.

14

Heaven-Scent Skunks

Lovebug and Bashful, two male skunks, came into our care late one summer from a southern animal sanctuary. The individual who raised them from tiny blind kittens believed that at their size, which was about half that of an adult when they were brought to us, they were ready for release.

"No," I said. "They're too young. We'll overwinter them and then allow them to go free."

I explained that young skunks take shelter with their mothers, learning from them how to survive the winter. It is, of course, possible that skunklets deprived of their mother will find proper shelter, but many such orphans die of exposure in an unsuitable den.

So I built them a cage attached to which was an insulated nesting box and Lovebug and Bashful took over the residence. In the beginning, however, the twins were not in a sleepy mood, which was normal during a time when there was no frost at night. But if they were not sleeping, they were hungry, consuming twice daily a container of food that included grapes, marshmallows, peanut butter sandwiches, cooked chicken, hamburger, and chocolate chip cookies. On that diet, the skunks grew and began to get fat. They slept a lot, but throughout winter they never went into a deep, prolonged sleep. This, of course, was because of the food we continued to give them.

They also remained docile, but, although siblings, there was a remarkable behavioral difference between them. Lovebug, so christened by Sharon, because he always demanded fuss, which included head scratching and stroking, was calm and inquisitive. On the other hand, Bashful, also named by Sharon, spent most of his time in the nesting box when people were around. If caught outside, however, he would dash back and forth inside the cage until in due course he realized that he could take shelter in the nesting box.

As usual, we had quite a number of visitors that autumn, all of whom were introduced to Lovebug and Bashful and, with rare exceptions, felt uneasy when in close proximity of the skunks, fearing the expected, "dreadful squirt."

To put them at ease, I would pick up Lovebug, sitting him bottom-first in the palm of my left hand, thumb and forefinger of my right hand raising him upright by the loose skin at the back of his head. Lovebug seemed to enjoy such attention and never once let loose even the tiniest drip of his potent defense fund.

In late October, Dr. Laurie Brown, our always helpful veterinarian, telephoned me to say that, for a change, she needed a little help, since she had one or more skunks that had decided to spend the winter under one part of her home. Perhaps Dr. Brown would not have called me if her unexpected rent-free tenants had not misbehaved a couple of times. Alas, they had! And no one likes to live in a dwelling that has been gassed by the juices of *Mephitis mephitis*.

Could I help? Of course! I got my large live-trap from the garage, showed Laurie how it worked, and gave her instructions on the manner in which a skunk should be carried once it got into the trap. Move slowly, I advised, and quietly. Then the skunk will behave sedately.

The first captive arrived the next day. It had behaved well. I picked the trap up by its handle — slowly, gently — and carried the prisoner to the building in which it would find suitable denning areas when released. If it did not like the lodging, of course, it could leave of its own free will and locate in any one of the many suitable and natural denning sites available on our forested property. As it happened, and although Dr. Brown and I had some difficulty opening the trap's gate and we made some noise in doing so, the skunk walked out to freedom, sniffed, then quickly disappeared under a pile of lumber. All was well.

Dr. Brown drove away with a slightly odorous truck, cage, and blanket.

The next day, I got another call. There was one more skunk in the trap. In fact, Dr. Brown and her family had unwittingly given shelter to four skunks: a mother and three young. All were live-trapped and brought to our sanctuary. All found shelter in our outbuilding; all dined every evening on the food that we put out for them. Come spring, the foursome left us, although they continue to show up now and then. But they are always well behaved.

In spring, when Lovebug and Bashful were ready to strike out on their own, both of them being hugely fat and healthy (having early on been inoculated against rabies and internal parasites), we opened up their cage. Did they dash out to find their freedom in the wild? Not a bit of it. Those two skunks knew when they were on to a good thing! They came out of their cage alright, but only to check their immediate environment. By afternoon, they were back inside, waiting for their customary ration of goodies.

Three weeks later, Bashful had at last taken to eating the succulent beetles and worms that teem on our property; and even Lovebug had by then almost stopped coming to get his evening snack, when he would grunt and sidle up to me, tilting his head sideways, like a cat, to be scratched under the chin. Although I knew that in due course he, too, would find his regular niche in the wild, I became very attached to Lovebug. I missed him when he stopped coming.

Why am I writing all this about six skunks? Because, as I've said before, most people are needlessly afraid of these docile animals. I have actually pushed out gently with my hand an Ontario skunk that had somehow entered an apartment hallway in suburban Toronto, thus preventing a wide-eyed policeman from shooting the animal (when the smell would have taken a long time to leave the building — not to mention the possibility of the bullet hitting a human).

If a person does not get excited, or move quickly, a skunk will not spray. Indeed, these animals seem to be quite reluctant to spray, only doing so when they feel themselves under attack, such as when a dog or a clumsy person provokes the squirts.

In fact, skunks are useful animals. They eat a great many insects and, when they dig holes in a lawn, they do so to reach the June beetle larvae that feed on the roots of grasses and plants. I have heard many a lawn-proud person curse *Mephitis mephitis* for spoiling the look of the lawn.

In reality, skunks should be praised for the habit. They keep the lawn healthy and, after all, it is easy to fill the cavities that they make.

15
Slick as a Weasel

Slick came into my care after I received a hysterical phone call from a woman who announced that she had a "filthy, smelly creature" in her basement. What was more, she claimed, the animal was threatening her cat and she was loath to open the basement door to let the cat out because she thought that the unwanted visitor would attack her.

When I had managed to calm her down, I asked questions about the fearsome beast. How long was it? About nine inches. What color was it? Brown. How high did it stand? About two inches off the ground. And it squeaked. The woman was describing a weasel, but, sight unseen, I had no means of determining just what kind of *Mustelid* we were dealing with. But I could safely say that weasels do not attack people or cats, although that comment did not pacify my caller.

In the event, I drove to the house and was ushered into the kitchen, where I met the basement door. I had brought a live-trap, but on explaining to the housewife that it might take a day or so for the weasel to enter the trap, she became quite excited, not so much because she was afraid, but because, she noted again, with emphasis and wrinkled nose: "The nasty beast reeks."

Well, I could not fault her for objecting to the odor. In truth, it permeated the kitchen, the distinctive scent confirming that the unwanted resident was, indeed, a member of the weasel family. All such animals are prone to pop out their quite powerful musk when disturbed, the most notorious and the champion stinkers of the Mustelid family being the skunks. An annoyed wolverine is a close second.

I explained some of this odorous biology to the lady, who seemed not at all interested in the aromas of other creatures, her whole attention being focused on her unwanted guest. So, while my guide hurriedly left the kitchen, I opened the basement door and started down the steps, trap in hand. About five minutes later I found the intruder. It was a very young least weasel, a little fellow that was only four inches long in the body and had a two-inch long tail. As I was soon to note, it was a male. He was cowering inside a cardboard box and was more than happy to climb on my open hand when I thrust it, slowly, into the container. Once in hand, I opened my shirt and Slick, as I was to call him, slipped inside and huddled against the warmth of my bare body. Returning upstairs, I called the lady of the house. On arrival in the kitchen she noted that the live-trap I was carrying was empty. I think she was about to run.

"What's the matter? Is it too dangerous?" she gasped.

Before I could say "no," that all was under control, Slick thrust his head out between two buttons of my shirt. As the tiny, inquisitive face fixed its black and beady eyes on his unwilling hostess, she shrieked and fled. Her shrill voice caused my passenger to dart back inside the shirt and to deposit a drop or two of his perfume, an event that caused me no discomfort, for by then I had been "odorized" by a wide variety of wild animals in need of care. A few weasel drops were quite supportable.

Least weasels are members of a large North American family that includes the pine marten, the fisher, the ermine (or stoat), the long-tailed weasel, the black-footed ferret (now almost extinct), the mink, the sea mink (extinct long ago), the western spotted skunk, the striped skunk, the river otter, the sea otter (now a threatened species), and, the largest of the Mustelid family, the wolverine and the badger.

With the exception of skunks and wolverines, which, although largely carnivorous, also eat vegetation, insects, and, indeed, almost anything else that is in any way edible — members of the weasel family are pure carnivores. Muste-lids eat a good deal more than their size might suggest. They metabolize rapidly and so must eat often, or die of starvation.

Mustelids emerged on earth some 39 million years ago.

There are sixty-five distinct species of Mustelids distributed in the majority of land areas of the world — they are *not* found in the West Indies, Madagascar, New Guinea, the Philippines, Australia, New Zealand, and Antarctica.

As matters turned out, Slick was a model foundling. He quickly accepted me as his foster parent, even to the extent of taking pieces of raw meat from my fingers without once biting the hand that fed him. Indeed, Slick became my constant companion when he was allowed to leave his temporary quarters so as to go walking with me in the forest, a treat that he enjoyed. However, he didn't always like to stay by my side, and on a few occasions, I thought that he had deserted me.

Following three of those instances, when after much frustration I would eventually coax him to me from wherever he had been hiding, I decided that the next time he did his vanishing act I would simply turn around and walk back home.

Well, several days later, Slick disappeared again. At first he had followed me dutifully, even though he stopped to play now and then, but after about three-quarters of an hour, he vanished. I was disappointed, but I reminded myself of my promise to simply walk away from him.

I told myself that Slick had done the right thing. He was a wild animal and he belonged to the forest and the river, not to me. Next I scolded myself for having allowed the weasel to develop such a close bond with me. Then I remembered that he was still too young to be on his own.

I kept on walking, willing myself to ignore the fact that I

had become very much attached to the happy little warrior, while at the same time I kept turning my head to see if he was catching up with me.

Half an hour later, when I was in sight of my clearing and now convinced that Slick would not come back, he popped up almost at my feet. Happy as usual, he scampered ahead, turned to look at me, squeaked, and ran on. I stopped, letting him go ahead; although his back was turned, he stopped and looked at me.

"Where did you go and how did you find me again after such a long time?" I asked rhetorically.

After some moments I answered my own question. Slick, like all wild mammals, had an acute sense of smell. Small as he was, his nose had picked up my spoor. He simply followed the odor of my footprints, being able to do so even through my boots (no matter how one tries to hide the scent that permeates the soles of one's boots or shoes, the keen noses of wild animals cannot be fooled).

Since Slick could move quickly, he had soon caught up with me after he got tired of whatever games he had been playing in the deep forest.

I now became somewhat concerned about Slick's reliance on me and I decided to coax him into taking long rambles on his own. It was easier said than done — he seemed to be able to read my mind! Finally, after a number of tries he seemed to be ready for release, even though he was still quite small.

So on a gorgeous, sunny morning in late May that was marred only by black flies, mosquitoes, deer flies, and horse-flies, all of which sought to dine on the hairless, exposed parts of my body, but yet avoided Slick and his self-impregnated repellent, we left the house and headed toward the forest.

At first I carried my small companion, taking him across the clearing, but soon after reaching the woods I put him down in an area of heavy underbrush. As usual, he darted into the thick of it, but unlike other occasions when after about ten minutes he would come back to me, this time he was still absent forty-five minutes later. I called him, uttered my very poor imitation of a weasel call, and tried to walk through the tangled area into which he had disappeared. All I got for my trouble was a number of fly bites.

Once again, I thought that Slick was ready to take his place in the wild. I turned around and started for home, but had only covered about sixty paces when a rapidly moving, agitated, squealing Slick ran to me, climbed one of my legs, and sought refuge inside my shirt. There, unquestionably in revenge, he popped his Mustelid cork and gave us both a good spray.

Twice more I had to walk away to teach him to come to me when I called, but by the third time he learned that when I called him he was to come to me. And so we avoided any of those panic moments when he thought that I was leaving him.

Slick spent all summer and into late fall with me. By November, however, he was big and healthy enough to make his way in his own world, so he was released. But the little weasel continued to "come home" every now and then and if I was in that part of the forest that he considered to be his territory, he invariably detected my presence and came to say "hello" by climbing my leg and seeking to enter my clothing.

As usual when one raises juvenile wild animals, one worries

about them. I missed Slick. Would he survive the winter? Had he learned to hunt his own food during our frequent forest outings? Of course, Sharon was just as concerned. But we need not have worried. He did well, and he came to visit us on numerous occasions during the course of two years. After that we saw him rarely, for by then he was a handsome young male weasel whose favorite pastime, when he was not eating, was courting lady weasels.

16
"Vicious" Wolverines

The most feared and persecuted member of the weasel family is the wolverine (*Gulo gulo*). It is also the hungriest, hence its Latin name, which translated means "greedy, greedy," although it is not actually greedy. Instead, like all members of the Mustelid family, it metabolizes rapidly, so it must eat lots and often.

This large Mustelid has been accused of all manner of nasty tricks, ranging from attacks on humans to a supposed capacity for killing very large animals, such as full-grown moose. It has also wrongfully been accused of having enormous strength, a kind of muscle power that can subdue even a bear, and it is often accused of eating the bodies of the people that it is supposed to have killed.

All of those "vicious" characteristics are the kind of nonsense that emerges when woodsmen huddle around a campfire at night and vie with each other in an effort to spin the tallest tales. In fact, there is absolutely no documented report of a wolverine attacking a human. But there have been a very great number of reports of humans killing wolverines: all of which are true!

I recall a sunny morning in May in the northern regions of British Columbia. I was sitting on a deadfall log resting after a hard climb and watching the tumbling waters of a mountain stream. Birds, especially a nearby varied thrush, made the morning musical, while the scent of evergreen needles perfumed my immediate environment. I was being idle, simply enjoying the morning and my surroundings.

It was perhaps my stillness that caused a female wolverine to walk within a few feet of me as she headed for the creek to quench her thirst. And undoubtedly because it copied its mother's serenity, one of her two kits also came trundling along within a yard of me. It joined its mother at the water's edge, but the second kit remained about twenty feet away, behind me and to the side, quite obviously afraid of the scent and sight of the first human it had ever seen. I had moved my head slightly, so I could keep the youngster within the sphere of my peripheral sight while at the same time watching the female and her bolder offspring.

The frightened youngster began to snarl, a loud but not very intimidating sound, yet one that could instill fear in some people. The sound of the kit's husky complaints reached its mother immediately. She turned her head, looked at her nervous offspring, grunted once, and then continued to suck up more water. The frightened kit, evidently reassured, advanced slowly but kept about four feet away from me and soon thereafter stood alongside the female.

Some minutes later the wolverine turned away from the stream, shook her fur, licked each kit, and set off down-creek, followed by the youngsters. The "vicious" creature knew perfectly well that I was nearby, but she completely ignored me.

That female *Gulo gulo* was the fifth of her kind I had seen over a period of eighteen years (I am not counting the two kits) and although at each sighting I had been relatively close to each animal, I have never been threatened. Three of the five wolverines lost no time in running away. The fourth, a female without young that I found cleaning up the remains of a cougar kill, did not run. Instead, staring at me, she growled ferociously, showing her impressive fangs, but she did not attempt to charge and continued eating when I ignored her growl. The fifth, as noted, ignored me.

The yarns that seek to vilify the wolverine, as well as many other so-called dangerous wild animals, are derived from ignorance and from the inherent belief that wild animals want nothing better than to harm, or actually kill, people. In truth, however, although black and grizzly bears have attacked humans, killing some of them, such attacks usually arise when a bear is suddenly startled by a person, when a bear is ill, when a female believes her cubs are in danger, or when foolish people go too close to a feeding bruin so as to get a "nice picture" of the animal. Then, too, large ungulate bulls, such as moose and elk, can be dangerous during the breeding season if a person approaches too closely.

Wolverines, although not endowed with miraculous muscle power, are strong for their size, and they *can* be aggressive if provoked, but like the great majority of large carnivores, they respect those humans who show no fear of them, who do not seek to impose on them, or who do not try to kill them with a rifle bullet or a steel leg-hold trap.

Seen in profile, a wolverine shows off its heavy coat of long, coarse guard hairs that hide a thick, soft undercoat. Adults generally measure between three-and-a-half and four feet, the males being the larger — some of the latter may reach a length of fifty-four inches. Males usually weigh between thirty and thirty-eight pounds, rarely up to forty-five pounds, and their height at the shoulder varies between twelve and fifteen inches. The body is muscular, and the relatively short tail is bushy.

Wolverines can run fast over short distances — perhaps up to twenty miles an hour when need arises. They have thick legs and large paws, similar to those of bears, each of which has five sharp, curved claws that are partly retractable and allow the animal to climb trees.

I once examined a wolverine skull. For an animal of its size, it was massive, broad, and obviously very strong. The teeth were equally massive and well adapted for crushing bones, while its formidable fangs obviously serve to hold and quickly kill a prey animal, then, later, to tear meat from the carcass.

Unquestionably, wolverines would be quite capable of killing an unarmed person if they were so inclined, but the fact remains that despite all the stories, these members of the weasel family have never once attacked a human. Wolverines are omnivorous and probably spend more time scavenging the leftovers of other carnivores than they do hunting. Additionally, they eat large quantities of roots and berries, catch and eat mice, and even eat fish when these are stranded on shorelines following the spring thaw, when fast running rivers deposit detritus on the shores.

Although they have no fixed breeding period, females are sexually receptive once a year. Males, on the other hand, become sexually active in April and continue to be so until early September.

Like bears, female wolverines have what is referred to as delayed implantation, meaning that the fertilized eggs remain in the womb, but do not become implanted in the uterine wall until some time in January. The young, between two and five, are born between late March and the middle of April.

Newborn kits come into the world dressed in downy, cream-colored coats. They have the typical wolverine dark face mask and stubby little tails. The mother breastfeeds the kits for about nine weeks, then, by about the beginning of June, she weans them and starts giving them meat.

At this time the mother becomes very active, for her young develop rapidly and, like all of their kind, seem to be constantly hungry. The mother must spend a long time hunting or searching for carrion with which to feed herself and her always hungry and fast-growing young. When not eating, they play-fight, growling ferociously and often screaming when one or the other bites too hard.

By mid-September most young wolverines leave the den and follow their mother. They learn to hunt by observing their mother's tactics and gradually beginning to stalk and kill small mammals such as marmots and hares and even birds like grouse and ptarmigan. When a year old, the young wolverines are on their own.

At one time, wolverines were found across the entire northern regions of Canada, in parts of the extreme north of the continental United States, and Alaska and part of Siberia. Today, the wolverine is either extremely scarce, or entirely extinct in most of the more southerly regions of its historic range. Trapped for its fur, killed on sight by hunters, and driven out of its range by the clear-cutting of forests, this interesting animal may well be on the road to extinction.

17
The Quiet Browsers

Porcupines, like many other animals, are often looked upon as aggressive, destructive creatures that should be shot on sight. As usual, such a view of the humble "Porky" is based upon human ignorance, compounded by the belief held by a great many people that there are only two kinds of natural groups on the planet: those that are "good for us" and those that are "bad for us," as was pronounced by the witch burner of Salem, the Reverend Cotton Mather (1663–1728), who intoned: "If it is not useful, it is vicious!"

This kind of thinking has for centuries been causing us to despoil our planet, generation after generation believing that we are the masters of our environment and so can do no wrong. Again and again we discover too late that we have caused serious damage to our world by dumping poisons in our waters, by creating pollution, and, of course, by arrogantly deciding what aspect of Nature is good, and what aspect of her is bad.

In the fifteenth century there were over 4,000 species of mammals. Of those, 36 have become extinct and at least 120 are today in danger of extinction, such as the bison, which is hanging on by a thread. In 1600 there were more than 8,000 species of birds. Today at least 120 species are extinct.

As a species, we humans seem unable to free ourselves from the ideas of people like Cotton Mather, whose dictum we consciously or unconsciously accept. A long time ago I, too, followed that dictum. But what changed my mind was an English lawn at the back of a relative's house. George was proud of his garden and when I visited him one day, I was willy-nilly ushered outside so that I could see his wonderful grass. But, as soon as we stepped on the lawn, he let out a yell and dashed to a spot where, he raged, grew a dandelion plant.

"Damned weeds!" he cried.

George impressed me negatively. Thinking about him and his "damned weeds" some weeks later, I concluded that a weed is a plant the benefits of which (for humans) have not yet been discovered. Today, I apply that dictum to all of Nature — even to the tiniest and most humble organisms. And I remember some words penned in 1853 by Henry David Thoreau: "Every creature is better alive than dead, both men and moose and pine trees, as life is more beautiful than death."

I am often reminded of Thoreau's words when I see porcupines deliberately run down on the highways by uncaring fools, who contend that porcupines destroy the forests and are therefore bad.

The porcupine is neither aggressive nor is it harmful to its environment. If it is attacked, it seeks to avoid danger by climbing a tree; if caught on the ground, it naturally seeks to defend itself. Nature created this animal and made it a vegetarian that during winter browses on the bark and foliage of trees, and in doing so lets fall to the forest floor a shower of buds and tender twigs that are avidly eaten by snowshoe hares, grouse, voles, and a variety of other small mammals. At the same time, a treed porcupine produces a large number of droppings, which land around the tree trunk and add fertilizer to the soil.

In spring and summer, as soon as ground vegetation emerges, the porcupine feeds on plants of the forest floor, thinning bushy areas as it continues to produce its fertilizer pellets. Thus, like all of nature's creations, it takes its nourishment from the natural world. But it also returns necessary substances to the environment.

From a purely human standpoint, the porcupine damages trees in winter by girdling them. Nevertheless, many trees so girdled — perhaps most of them — recover, growing new branches on the lower part of the trunk where the bark has not been entirely removed. Of course, foresters consider such "tinkering" with their trees to be an abomination, but I like to point out that the trees and the porcupines have existed side by side and in harmony for a great many thousands of years, long, long before the arrival of foresters and lakeside cottage owners.

There is no doubt that in more recent times porcupines have become overpopulated and so are, indeed, responsible for some forestal damage; but, here again, the fault lies with human behavior, rather than with the porcupines. By clear-cutting forests, by drastically thinning out the trees, or by almost entirely eliminating in south-central forest regions the porcupine's natural predators — such animals as the wolverine, the fisher, and the coyote — humans have allowed porcupine numbers to climb.

The overpopulation of an animal that has only one young a year and is easy prey for its predators, especially during its infancy, is a rarity in undisturbed environments. Only when humans interfere by removing what is thought to be a "pest" species, and at the same time trapping the fur bearers that are the "pest's" natural control, is the opportunity created for the overpopulation of the so-called destructive animals.

Incidentally, to prevent porcupines from gnawing on tool handles, plywood, and a variety of other items found around the cottage or home, use a salt block. Most chewing by porcupines occurs in spring when the animals are looking to replenish the salt levels in their bodies. Axe handles and other tools carry impregnated in their wood the salt from a human's hands, while plywood contains other kinds of salts, some of which may be lethal to the animal. A salt block placed in a particular location will last a long time and will surely divert a porcupine away from household items. In addition, many other wild creatures will take advantage of the salt, such as squirrels, chipmunks, hares, and rabbits.

Porcupines, as far as I am concerned, are useful residents of our forests and interesting animals if one gets to know them. Some years ago I delivered a baby porcupine by cesarian section when its mother was killed. I called him Spike and found him loving and gentle. He kept his quills tight against his body when I carried him and only occasionally did I get accidentally spiked.

I still remember Spike, and how, after I dried him off and felt his still rubbery quills, he sought to nurse from one of my fingers. Later, when I had fed him a balanced formula, I weighed him. Deducting almost three ounces of formula, he tipped the scales at twenty ounces. And I measured him. From his blunt little nose, to the end of his quilly tail, he measured eight-and-one-quarter inches. His body was covered in long, shiny black hairs among which one-inch-long yellow quills bristled, although at first the little spikes were soft and lacked the barbed tips.

Since I was the first living thing that Spike saw when he emerged into the world, he decided that I was his mother and, within minutes of being rid of the birth moisture, he started to climb up one of my legs, his tiny feet already nicely equipped with strong, black claws: four on the forefeet, and five on the back. Helping him upward, I allowed him to perch on my shoulder, whereupon he began to squeal in my ear as he attempted to suck its lobe.

Fifteen minutes later I silenced the squealing infant with a bottle of formula. After his feed, he went to sleep in a cardboard box.

Spike remained with me for four years. He grew up to weigh (at last weigh-in, when he was two years old) thirty-five pounds, which made him about ten pounds heavier than most male porcupines, no doubt because he had plenty of nourishment during his growing years.

In June 1995, we accepted the care of another young porcupine, a female whose mother had been killed by a car. She was less than one-quarter grown and her spikes were still somewhat soft and scarce. We named her Prickles.

As expected, our new ward was gentle. We kept her in a long, low cage that was fitted with a good nesting box. From the first, Prickles was quiet and unafraid. She was past the sucking stage, but she nevertheless enjoyed, and survived on, a diet of bitch's milk formula that was well laced with human infant pabulum, and also contained a good spoonful of human-infant strawberry puree. On this diet Prickles thrived.

About every other day I would dig up a solid bunch of dandelions and put it in the little porcupine's cage together with some tender branches of balsam firs. She liked that green stuff, but she did not eat a lot of it, for she was far more interested in the twice-daily formula feeds.

Prickles remained docile, but somewhat shy. Like all of her kind, she moved slowly when not disturbed and, on those occasions when I was feeding her, or cleaning her cage, she would sniff my fingers to make sure I was one of her two "mothers," and then she would begin to eat.

In July, we decided that Prickles was big enough and old enough to find her way in her own world, so we opened the cage. She did not rush to get out! Indeed, it must have been dark when she did finally emerge.

Once free, however, she did not go very far, a fact that, ensconsed in the nearby forest, she announced by uttering the husky, soft grunts of her kind. When I was in the area, I would answer her and although my grunts were not as genuine as those of other porcupines, she responded to them. In fact, for the next four weeks, she continued to respond to my calls every evening and she would amble out of the trees, sniff me, then go to her dish of formula, which she lapped up until all was gone. That done, and very slowly and gently, she would amble away.

After the start of her fifth week of freedom, she stopped visiting with us, opting instead for the life of the seasoned porcupine. We still miss her, but we are happy that she has found sanctuary on our property.

Porcupines live right across North America and are absent only from Newfoundland, northern Labrador, and the tundra of the Northwest Territories. Also, they have been made extinct, or nearly so, in extreme southern Ontario and similar regions in the United States.

Like all animals that discommode the human species, porcupines are quite high on the list of mammals to be persecuted. It does no good to say that these docile, slow-moving creatures are peaceable unless attacked; it does no good to mention that they are of benefit to the forests because they thin out dense sections of saplings, especially balsam firs that have become wild-seeded in foolishly clear-cut areas that once contained white pines and other trees. And it does no good to explain that the porcupine is a natural being created by evolution for particular purposes, a companion of trees and an integral part of its ecosystem.

I like porcupines! But then, I like all animals — with the exception of certain brands of my own kind, that is. I put out salt blocks at various strategic locations on our property and we enjoy watching the bristly lumps as they lick up their salt ration. Rising on their hind legs and staring at us as we walk toward them, they allow us to approach to within three or four or five feet before they slowly turn around and waddle away.

18
Paddy the Beaver

A number of years ago, I was charting a lake and its surrounding forests in a region north of Bancroft, Ontario. One night, soon after I had returned to my shoreline campsite at sunset, I heard the piercing whistle of a red-shouldered hawk.

Walking to the water's edge, I looked up and soon sighted the sturdy bird of prey as it swept back and forth above a large beaver lodge. The bird was circling, going lower with each pass. Focusing the field glasses on the tall structure of sticks and mud, I couldn't see anything that might be of interest to the hawk. However, on searching the nearby shore, which was dressed in a profusion of arrow-weed, I saw a large tree stump. As I focused on it, the hawk flew into the field of vision. Its stoop was lower. It was clearly concentrating on the stump.

At first all I could see were a few sprouting weeds and a small seedling poplar that grew out of a crack in the wood. But turning the glasses on the stump, which was about two feet high, I saw a dark, still ball of fur. It was a tiny beaver kit. Then I remembered that two days earlier, soon after my arrival, I had found the remains of a female beaver.

Large tracks in the sand around the remains had identified a wolf, which had obviously killed the beaver. There hadn't been much left of the animal, but on a patch of skin about five inches long by some three inches wide I had noticed a breast nipple that in life had been engorged by milk.

Having studied the natural world for more than half a lifetime, I had long ago accepted the fact that predators such as wolves have to kill in order to survive. It is nature's way. Indeed, I had also concluded at the same time that no organism — human or otherwise — can survive on the planet without feeding off living things (in this regard, plants are, of course, living things). So, despite feeling concern for the dead mother beaver, and, I must admit, feeling angry with the wolf that had made the kill, I nevertheless considered my find to be just one more story to be read in the book of Nature: an animal had died so that another could have life. But as I watched the hawk sweep over the tiny beaver, coming so low that its wings almost brushed the cowering shape, I was on this occasion unable to stand by idly while nature took its course.

My canoe was at the water's edge, only about ten feet from where I stood and so, yelling to put the hawk off its stroke, I launched the boat and started paddling toward the stump's shoreline, taking two strokes at a time, then pounding the paddle against the bow of the cedar-strip canoe to make a loud booming sound that clearly disturbed the hawk. If the little beaver was still alive, I would reach it in time.

Moments later, the canoe scraped against the stump and I found myself looking into a doleful, anguished baby face out of which two black eyes stared at me apprehensively. Now I spoke quietly, uttering soft words delivered in a reassuring tone. Next, I reached slowly for the cringing little bundle. When my hand was only about two inches from the kit, I stopped it in mid-air and spoke more softly, soothingly. Carefully, I lowered my hand. It touched the matted fur and my fingers curled around the shriveled body. I crooned my silly words as I tightened my grip just enough to lift the orphan, which I now saw was a male.

The little beaver made no protest. It just stared at me and I could not decide whether its gaze was trusting, or whether it signaled that the tiny animal was resigned to dying. I undid my shirt and put the infant inside, against the left side of my body, so it could feel my warmth and my heartbeat, both of which sensations have an almost immediate calming effect on fearful infant animals. Sitting in the canoe, I began to gently stroke the kit's head and, as I was doing so, the hawk left the immediate area — but not before it uttered one more whistle.

The youngster responded to my soft touch. Moments

later, it began to suck on my shirt while making little sobbing noises. Now I had to get my ward to shore and prepare some milk for it.

As usual when I am intending to spend a long time doing field research, I had brought a good supply of powdered skim milk as well as a large container of powdered glucose, both of which were intended for my use, but were from that moment on reserved for the kit. Also, out of habit occasioned by numerous rescues of helpless young animals, I had also brought two eyedroppers, useful for dripping warm formula into starving babies' mouths.

Now, needing both hands to paddle, I left the orphan against my body and buttoned the shirt. Minutes later I beached the canoe and carried the beaver to my tent, where, after lighting a small alcohol stove I carried for emergencies (the kind fired by tablets), I warmed some milk to body temperature and prepared to load the eyedroppers. But first I wanted the kit to "know" my scent, so I took the infant from inside my shirt and brought him to my mouth. He smelled musky and sour, and there was an odor of mushrooms about him — no doubt from the fungi that grow within a damp lodge — and as I thrust out my tongue and licked his face and mouth, I noticed a small leech sucking blood from his right ear. But I continued licking face and mouth and head, wanting him to identify with me, to know that the creature in whose keeping he now was would care for him and comfort him.

Moments later I took a sip of the formula and brought the orphan to my mouth. He smelled the food at once and, when I allowed him to touch my lips with his own, started to suck before I was ready. Milk dribbled out of my mouth and my tongue was seized in a surprisingly strong grip. Soon after, however, my ward settled down and finished what formula I had in my mouth. Now I introduced him to the eyedropper and although I believe he would have preferred to continue drinking from my mouth, he soon settled to his meal.

That night, after I climbed into my sleeping bag, I put the beaver in with me after he had consumed his fourth feed since his rescue. During the night, he repaid my attention by wetting me and by exercising his bowels on my stomach.

However, as time was to tell, Paddy, as I christened him after he showed me that he had a temper if he did not immediately get his way, thrived to the point that I was able to release him into his family's lake, where his large and grumpy father immediately took him in hand.

I studied that colony right up to freeze-up. It consisted of the large male, a young female — probably a two-year-old — and three yearlings. But Paddy appeared to be the only survivor of that year's litter.

In time, I wrote a book about Paddy. And although many years have passed since my friendship with him and his family, he continues to have a special place in my memory.

19
The Study of Life

Not long ago I received a letter from a high school student who had informed her science teacher that she was no longer going to dissect animals that had been expressly killed for study purposes. Among the many good points that she made was the fact that with the availability of a number of fine alternatives, it is no longer necessary to kill animals in order to study the physiology of life.

The killing of animals for dissection continues, however. What an irony! We look at death and we believe that we are studying life!

I recall that soon after completing four years of biological study, during which I majored in mammalogy, I became frustrated with certain aspects of the science and decided to pursue my own course while earning a living as a writer. I did not, however, abandon biology, which is to me the most fascinating of all the sciences because those of us who follow the discipline have the opportunity to learn so much about ourselves. But I did strike out on my own, becoming an academic maverick and pursuing my further studies in the field, learning by firsthand observation and in the process discovering that textbooks at times contain an awful lot of nonsense.

During my formal studies, as every biologist must do, I went through the classroom exercises, sat through monotonous lectures, and was led along a pathway liberally paved with the cadavers of experimental animals and signposted by their disassembled parts: the blood, viscera, bones, and skin that had once belonged to a veritable host of sentient creatures.

With one noteworthy exception, all my professors and tutors sought to teach me about life by forcing me to study death, yet I knew from my own firsthand experience that Nature is splendidly alive and continuous, despite the fact that its constituent entities are individually mortal.

I felt then, and I do now, that it is not possible to study life by dissection, just as it is impossible to learn anything truly worthwhile about the behavior of an organism by observing it in restricted captivity. This is not to say that future biologists should spend all their time in the field; nor do I mean to imply that classroom and laboratory study is worthless. Quite to the contrary: without the imposed disciplines of academic life I could not have learned to ask the right questions when observing in the field, nor how to seek the answers diligently and constructively. Biology as a science is as important to me today as it ever was, yet I feel that virtually all of the sciences have become too rigid and inward looking, and that, in fact, the tails are wagging the dogs — as the saying goes. A number of biologists of my acquaintance pursue their individual specialties in tunnels within which they rarely look to left or right. They have become clinicians; they are more concerned about the good opinion of their colleagues than they are about the real content of their researches, clinging to the credo: "publish or perish."

The late Charles Elton, the well-known English ecologist, came to this conclusion long before I did when he wrote in 1927 that the discoveries of Darwin ". . . himself a magnificent field naturalist, had the remarkable effect of sending the whole zoological world flocking indoors, where they remained hard at work for fifty years or more, and whence they are now beginning to put forth cautious heads again into the open air."

Well, as far as I can determine, there are still far too many heads that remain cautious when it comes to the study of life in the open air.

It seems that during the last century many scientists have come to regard themselves as a breed apart, a chosen elite for whom the curiosity of the layman is a nuisance, perhaps even an impertinence. The result of this attitude is that although we are living in the most enlightened scientific time in our history, the average person remains singularly ill-informed where Nature is concerned, while those young people who elect to pursue a career in biology become programmed to think of life as being expendable, something that can be clinically analyzed with scalpels and microscopes. This view, of course, predominates in high schools where, I believe, it is all the more serious because it is producing whole generations who have little or no respect for life; or else, it is so disgusting, that many sensitive young people turn away from the study of biology.

The result of such attitudes is reflected in the fact that far too many people think of Nature as being a chattel of humankind. This causes them to calmly accept the political-economic view that says, in effect, that the earth is a place on which to build more suburbs, parking lots, factories, and highways while the forests are being devastated, the land itself plundered for its "resources," the air polluted, and the ether punctured by our exhausts.

Thus, while some individuals hold life in high esteem, respecting the right of all species to borrow some sunshine from it for a time, the majority of humans are becoming more self-seeking and less and less concerned with the value of life, or with the price that will one day have to be paid for its abuse.

If biology has one major failure, it is this: those of us who have devoted ourselves to the science have by default allowed ignorance to grow unchecked while our environment is being assaulted as never before. No one of us willingly accepts individual responsibility for this state of affairs, but, collectively, we are all at fault, for we have allowed it to happen.

For all of the above reasons, I was greatly encouraged

recently when a small number of my neighbors came to see me to ask for advice on forming a field-naturalists group. I was delighted to assist and even more delighted when, after relatively little advertising, about sixty residents turned up at the founding meeting.

Alas, disappointment was soon to follow! It turned out that the great majority of the "field naturalists" were mostly interested in bird watching and social entertainment and were too timid to lock horns with government officials in order to seek some sensible conservation measures in their neighborhood.

I am certainly not opposed to bird watching. Indeed, I watch birds on a daily basis, but over the years I have noted that many bird-watching aficionados tend to forget that birds need habitats and thus they do not realize the problems that daily attack the natural environment.

Over the years I have learned that there are two kinds of bird watchers. The one kind enjoys watching birds as a whole and at the same time is careful — while seeking to "collect" one more special bird for their "life's lists" — not to trample down the undergrowth, nor to destroy other parts of the natural world that may be home to ground nesters, tree dwellers, or small mammals. The other kind has no such regard.

Bird watchers in the former category are good for the environment and, besides, many, if not the majority, learn about biology while enjoying the birds. Some bird watchers, like John James Audubon (1785–1851), who painted and studied the birds of North America, have contributed greatly to the science of ornithology.

Nevertheless, while being aware of the major contributions

made by Audubon, Roger Tory Peterson, Colin Harrison, and many others, it should not be supposed that any one individual, or, indeed, group of individuals, can ever hope to discover all that there is to know about the biology of birds or of their habitats.

The study of birds should always be joined with the study of natural life as a whole, since in Nature everything is connected to everything else: Without trees and shrubs and grasses there can be no life, and without the other living things — reptiles, birds, mammals, insects, bacteria, fungi, slime molds, and others — there cannot be trees and shrubs and grasses.

In my own case, I find myself in full agreement with Dr. Lewis Thomas, a physician–philosopher who wrote in *Lives of Cell*: "It is nice to think that there are so many unsolved puzzles ahead for biology, although I wonder whether we will ever find enough graduate students."

We were recently faced by an unsolved puzzle when we were asked to look after a male scarlet tanager that had lost all its tail feathers. The bird, found in a Toronto, Ontario, street, was in all other ways healthy, but without its tail feathers — its rudder. It could not fly because it could not "steer." It reminded me of an automobile driver whose vehicle had no steering wheel! When it came to us, it was ravenously hungry because its well-meaning rescuers had sought to feed it with bread soaked in milk instead of putting it on a proper diet.

Although over the years we have successfully rehabilitated a number of birds that in one way or another had been in urgent need of care, we had never had experience with tanagers, although the bird's robust beak suggested that a meat diet of some kind was indicated. At first, seeking advice from an expert bird rehabilitator, I was told to feed the bird a variety of items, but it would not eat any of the recommended foods.

Then we tried our own mixture: boiled egg yoke, ground beef, pieces of apple, grapes, and vitamins. Success! Suffice it to say that the tanager thrived, but it took two full months before it had grown a proper tail. At this point it was released and I watched it as it rose over the trees and headed south.

I make reference to the tanager's story not because it ended successfully, but because, puzzling though it may have been, it points to the fact that all living things are individuals. It is my experience that individuality is the norm in all aspects of nature. In all probability another tanager would have thrived on the diet recommended by the bird rehabilitator, but "our" bird preferred what we offered it.

In the matter of individuality, I have for some years now offered a reward of $100 for anyone who can find me two identical leaves on the same tree, or two identical tree trunks, or two identical animals. So far, I have not had any takers.

20
Lessons from Ants

It seems to me that there are times when it is left to the humble creatures of the world to teach us humans a lesson in humility. At least, there have been many such times for me. Occasions when, more out of habit than curiosity, I look casually at some organism or object and find myself suddenly engrossed by what I see and learn.

It happened like that one day when I paused to look at a large anthill the indefatigable little insects had built on the edge of a forest clearing, a mound of fine, well-worked soil that rose exactly eighteen inches from the ground and had a base of twenty-seven inches.

Small, red-black ants inhabited the interior of the mound and, when I poked a thin, exploratory stick a few inches into the side of the hill, the occupants boiled out, streams of them, emerging through different entrances. Each ant was about three-eighths of an inch long. All emerged with their pincers wide, seeking the enemy that had dared to disturb their fortress. After two minutes, since nothing else attacked their home, the ants settled down. Most of them re-entered the hill, others busied themselves in tidying up, filling in spaces, and removing dead leaves and twigs from the upper part of the mound.

Nearby, I spotted a dead June bug, or May beetle (*Phyllopha aga fusca*), and picked it up. It was still fresh — it had probably crashed into a tree or heavy branch — so I tossed it on the anthill. I timed events. Within thirteen seconds eighteen ants had clustered around the beetle and began the task of moving it. Seconds later a veritable host of ants emerged and scurried to help in the task. Their efforts made me think of the building of the great Egyptian pyramids. The beetle bulked greater than one hundred times the estimated total weight of all the ants, yet, infinitely slowly, they began to move it.

Moments later, more help came. At the response of some mysterious scent emitted by the workers, hundreds more ants emerged from the hill's various tunnels and fell upon the beetle. Fascinated, I forgot to time the next event, but in what I estimated as thirty or forty seconds, the beetle was dismembered and "drawn and quartered," each bit of its body carried into the hill.

When all except about a dozen ants remained outside the hill, I was about to leave when I noticed the grass that covered the mound. Not sure at first about what drew my attention to it, I stared for some time. It finally dawned on me that the grass on the mound was somewhat different than the grass of the surrounding area, yet I could not determine what it was. The growth was fresh, light green, and, when I plucked a couple of stems, tender in comparison to the grass that surrounded the hill. It was between three and four inches high and, I thought idly, resembled more a planted crop than a haphazardly seeded growth. On the heels of that thought, I realized that the hill grass was, indeed, a planted crop, and a well-tended one at that.

Looking more closely, I saw a number of individual ants cutting down stems of grass and hauling them into the hill. Other ants appeared to be cleaning the mound of bits of dead leaves, twigs, and other useless items that had fallen on the hill or been blown there. Since that time, I have seen a number of such anthills; on every one the ants farm grass.

Ants of another species that have fascinated me for a long time are also small, perhaps three-eighths of an inch long, but they are quite ferocious and capable of raiding the nests of large carpenter ants and stealing the larvae, which they carry away to their nests and there allow the bigger larvae to hatch with their own young. Afterward, they use the big ants as slaves.

My first experience of this behavior took place some thirty years ago after I noticed a stream of little red ants returning to their nest, which had been established under a flat rock. Each ant was carrying a large and heavy black ant larva. When I traced the raiders to their abode, I saw that other ants, which had evidently already brought home the black ant larvae, were setting out again, traveling in the opposite direction of those that were returning loaded.

Following the outward line while wondering how it was that the large ants allowed the midgets to steal their future young, I soon came to the ant nest, which was underground. Outside the main entrance there was chaos! The large ants milled around, greatly agitated, but they were not attacking the little red ants, each of which entered the alien nest and soon after returned to the surface with a large, fat larva in its mouth.

I was amazed. Not only because the little ants were raiding the black ants, but because the latter allowed their tiny enemies to get away with their raiding. How could that be?

Later I learned that the red ants possess what can only be described as a disorienting scent. Evidently, upon the discharge of the stupefying "drug," the black ants, while frantic, are unable to determine what is happening, despite the fact that they are aware that something is radically wrong.

On the occasion of my first observation of slave-making behavior, I waited until the raiders had finished kidnapping the black ant larvae and I lifted the flat rock under which was the nest. Despite the fiery behavior of the tiny guardians, who climbed up my pant legs and bit me, each tiny chomp feeling as though a red-hot spark had somehow traveled up my limbs, I photographed the larvae. The picture shows the large black ant larvae and the very small red ant larvae.

Over the years I have studied quite a number of different

species of ants and I am continually amazed by their behavior as well as by their many abilities, such as the scent that a scout lays while returning to the nest after finding a source of food, a trail that allows all the other ants of the colony to find their way to the site. Ants also have a built-in compass that lets them find their way almost anywhere, but the device must be oriented to the sun. After a long winter of hibernation, all the emerging ants must rotate their bodies so as to "set" their compasses.

On one occasion, following a line of red ants from their nest to their quarry, I was surprised to see that they had either found, or hunted, the larva of a wood-boring beetle, a large, fat-headed creature that was alive, but the prey of at least a hundred red ants. It took those midget warriors an hour and six minutes to push and pull the monster food source to their nest.

Ants are related to wasps, sharing such physical characteristics as the thin waists and the hard, waterproof outer skin that allows them to move about above ground during wet weather, or in the heat of summer without losing any of their moisture.

The homes of ants vary considerably. Some species live in hills that are between two and three feet tall; others live under rocks; yet others make tunnels and chambers by boring into the wood of trees as well as into the wood of human habitations. But the most indefatigable ants are the leaf-cutters: they burrow into the soil, making galleries that can go down as deep as six feet and encompass an area of more than two thousand square feet. Leaf-cutters cannot break down celllose, but they can absorb the honeydew.

It occurs to me now that if these hardy, clever insects ever become as large as tigers, they will surely take over the world!

21
The Silk Weavers

When I was eight years old, I fell in love with spiders. I made their acquaintance in one of a series of deep and interesting caves in Barcelona's Parque Guell, a large preserve donated to the city by the Count of Guell. The northern entrance of the woodlands was within a half hour's walk from my home and, when not captive by school or parents, I used to haunt the caverns.

In the largest of these caverns I stored such important things as a digging trowel, glass jars with lids, candles, and matchboxes, the kind that used to have striking paper on both sides and little sliding drawers that contained wooden matches. When empty, these matchboxes were ideal for temporarily housing small insect specimens that were usually released in our large back garden. If interesting enough to keep, however, some were for a time housed in a garden shed, a large room in which had been assigned to me by my father at my mother's behest so as to keep my "finds" outside of her domain. Mother was not enamored with insects, dead mice, a nice collection of dried horse and donkey droppings, feathers, bones, and, my prize specimen for a time, a dead, well-dried bat.

My first arachnid friend was a large female wolf spider, which, as I recall, was quite hairy, slightly more than one inch long, and carrying all of her many spiderlings on her back. I was so fascinated with my prize that I immediately popped her in a glass jar, secured the lid, and ran almost all the way to our home, which I usually entered through a stout door that was inset in one wall of our garden. On that occasion, however, I was so excited and anxious to settle my new ward that I went in through the front door just as my mother was about to go out.

Mother, who tried hard to show interest in my doings, asked what kind of object was moving in the jar. I proudly raised the container so that she could see Arana (Spanish for spider), whom I had already christened. I can still see my mother's face.

"My God!" she cried. "That's a tarantula! Flush the nasty thing down the toilet!"

That was in August 1930, exactly four weeks before my ninth birthday. Until that time, nobody had told me that wolf spiders were supposed to be nasty, aggressive creatures that loved to bite humans and so inject into their blood the venom that many years before my birth had given rise to the colloquial name, *tarantula*.

The name comes from Taranto, Italy, and was bestowed on the Mediterranean region wolf spider when people believed that if bitten by the spider they could cure themselves by dancing frantically. Such antics eventually gave rise to the tarantula dance, but history does not say if any Taranto resident was ever bitten by a wolf spider, and, certainly, there are no records of people dying from its bite. As a result, however, any large wolf spider almost anywhere in North America and especially in South America — where in the tropics unaggressive wolf spiders can reach a length of four inches — is referred to as a Tarantula.

The true scientific name of the so-called tarantula is *Lycosa*, which is applied to the family of large to medium spiders. Some of these run over the ground hunting their prey; others burrow underground and catch their food at the entrance to their tunnels; and yet others make funnel-shaped webs into which insects fall and are immediately taken by the watchful spider. Female *Lycosae* adhere their egg cases to their spinnerets — the tubes from which the silk is spun — and carry them around for several weeks; then, just before the spiderlings are ready to leave their shelter, the mother rips open the silken pouch, allowing the young to emerge. The spiderlings crawl out and quickly climb on the mother's back. Because a female wolf spider may lay more than one hundred eggs, the spider-lings ride on each other's backs, in layers. In due course the young cling to their mother's underside for six or seven days, then they gradually drop off and make their own way in the world.

Although I was too young to appreciate the extraordinary manner in which the spiderlings first rode with their mother and then slipped away from the cage in which I had kept the female, I was amazed by the event. And I still recall that after the tiny spiders had all disppeared and I let their mother go free in our garden, I told one of my teachers about the experience. He did not believe me and, as a punishment, he ordered me to write an essay that would explain the reasons for lying to him!

Since that long ago time, I have had a great deal to do with spiders and other insects. Despite the fact that some of our guests react with horror when entering the bathroom and discovering a spider in the wash basin, I do not kill any arachnids that find their way into our home, and I will not allow anyone else to do so. Like most "creepy-crawly" creatures, spiders have been given a bad press for many centuries, yet they are extremely useful, environmentally friendly animals, the majority of which prey actively on insect pests. A few, apart from taking insects, also hunt tiny minnows and even other spiders, for all spiders are carnivorous.

I particularly like the little crab spiders, *Thomisidae*, which lie quietly in ambush on plants or on the inside window panes of our house, especially in the winter. If prey comes within reach of the vigilant little hunter, it gets caught in a flash by the spider's strong front legs and thereafter is bitten and becomes paralyzed. The victim is then sucked dry through minute bite holes inflicted by the captor.

I especially appreciate the crab spiders during autumn, when no matter how we try to exclude flies from the house, they somehow enter. But those that we miss with the swatter are soon disposed of by our friendly little spiders.

I have not actually counted the numbers of spiders of different species that I have studied and befriended, but I know that had I done so, my total would be woefully low compared to the more than 35,000 different species so far identified. And it is almost certain that a good many more new species will become known in the future, for these interesting creatures have colonized every part of the earth except Antarctica and the polar regions.

Individually, spiders can live almost anywhere. They reside in houses, in outbuildings, under rocks, on trees, shrubs, small plants, lawns, in flowers, and in underground or above ground caves. A few species, like the so-called dock spider, can walk on water as well as they can walk on land. The dock spider is actually a wolf spider, *Pardosa amentada*.

A few years ago I captured a male *Pardosa* and put it in a small pond on my property that always contains numerous kinds of surface insects. I hoped to be able to watch the spider's behavior, but I had a feeling that it would probably leave within minutes of its transfer. As it happened, however, the *Pardosa* stayed all summer long, undoubtedly because of the many prey insects that were available to it; I watched many times as it skillfully provided for itself.

Many people dislike spiders, and the majority of such

individuals will kill them if they encounter them in their homes, mistakenly believing that these insects bite people and inject poison into their victims.

In fact, there are only a very few species of spiders that are capable of breaking through tough human skin — and the great majority of these live in the tropics. Some of them do bite and they do inject poison in their victims. In North America the most poisonous spider is the black widow (*Latrodectus mactans*), although those that live in the northern half of the continent tend to be quite small and are probably unable to bite through human skin. Certainly, some years ago, while in British Columbia, I had the good fortune of finding three black widows at different times. Although I handled them repeatedly, I was not bitten.

An unusual spider is *Scytodes*, or spitting spider, which immobilizes its prey by spitting glue at it. When the target animal is hit by the sticky liquid, it is pinned to the ground, or rock, and the spitter then injects poison into it, killing it and eating it, the venom having no effect on the spider. *Scytodes* are mostly tropical, but one species, *Scytodes thoracica*, lives in southwestern United States.

Another unusual spider is the *Dolomedes*, the female of which species is seen more often than the male because, like some other spider species, the female eats her mate the instant they conclude the nuptial act. Why this occurs is not known. Probably such behavior acts as a natural control and may ensure that only the fittest males get to mate and so pass on their genes for future generations.

At least some male *Dolomedes*, however, manage to survive

the deadly mating ritual. Such a male first catches an insect, wraps it in silk, and, when his chosen female signals that he may approach her, he carries the gift in his jaws and makes the offering. While his spouse is busy removing the silk from her present and eating the offering, the male mates with her and then scurries away before she has finished munching!

A number of species of spiders can change color at will. Two kinds of crab spiders, *Misumena vatia* and *Thomisius onustus*, change the color of their abdomens — which are white in the first species, and yellow in the second — to correspond to the white or yellow blossoms on which they sit while waiting for an insect to come near them. Such camouflage, of course, confuses their prey and also protects the spiders from their enemies.

When it comes to weaving and manufacturing fibers, spiders are the champions! One species, *Nephila clavipes*, found in southern United States and in the tropics, makes a huge web — up to thirty-nine inches in diameter — with silk that is rated as the strongest natural fiber known.

All web spiders produce silk from their abdominal glands, and they can make different kinds of it: smooth, nonsticky silk for the sustaining frames of their webs, or sticky silk on which to trap insects, or silk from which they make sacks to protect their eggs.

The "mechanics" of silk making are complex but fascinating. Briefly, silk is a fiber-like protein that is ejected from little taps at the end of a spider's spinnerets. The silk comes out liquid, but hardens immediately on contact with the air. So thin that a single strand is most often invisible to the human eye, this material is yet strong and incredibly elastic; one line is able to stretch as much as one-quarter of its length before it breaks.

From spring to late autumn we have a variety of small spiders active in the house, their territories being window ledges, plants, little holes in woodwork, or the basement in slight indentations between cement blocks. We are by no means inundated with arachnids, but between the upstairs, the downstairs, and the basement we have, on average, about two dozen, the majority being not much longer than five-sixteenths of an inch.

We always welcome the spring emergence of our friendly little spider flycatchers, even at those times when one of them swings across a room on a silken thread to land on head or shoulder and from there to gently climb on an extended index finger before it quickly launches itself at a plant or window glass, always maintaining its balance and landing feet first.

Sharon has a number of Christmas cactuses that bloom four or five times a year. These plants (*Zygocactus truncatus*) are also called Crab cactuses, a name that puzzles a lot of people since neither the pulpy, gently spiked leaves nor the gorgeous pink or white blooms resemble crabs.

Being of a somewhat curious disposition, I spent some time trying to find the origin of the plant's second name. First I looked carefully at the leaves and flowers, but I could find no resemblance to crabs. Next I searched the literature: another blank. I gave up. Yet, each time that I was about to pass a cactus, I would stop and stare at it briefly, being not quite willing to admit defeat.

One morning in August, struck by the magnificent display of deep pink blossoms that festooned the largest cactus, I stopped to admire it, noting, as I bent over the gorgeous flowers, that two flies were busy sipping nectar from the blossoms. That was not an unusual event. I had witnessed it many times over the years, for living as we do surrounded by forests, flies of one kind or another always find a way into the house.

What startled me, however, was the emergence of a tiny crab spider that scuttled upward and along the outside of the flower inside of which the fly was lapping honeydew.

On reaching the edge of the petal, the spider stopped. It became immobile. The fly continued to lap honeydew, unaware of the spider. A while later, having evidently emptied the nectar supply, the fly backed out of the flower, straightened up, and paused on the petal's rim, there to clean itself. It was not aware that it had stopped about three-eighths of an inch away from the spider. I was about to leave quietly so as to go and get my camera to photograph the scene when the immobile spider flashed into action. Darting upward, its two front legs extended, it imprisoned the fly.

I timed the events. The crab spider first drilled a minute hole in the prey's body, then it pumped digestive fluid into the fly in enough quantity and with enough pressure to force the victim's "juices" to emerge through the hole, thus allowing the spider to lap up every last morsel of the fly's internal organs.

The miniature but rather gruesome operation took one minute and thirty-four seconds, after which, evidently satisfied, the spider disappeared among the branches of the cactus. I then got a magnifying glass and examined the remains. Intriguingly, the carcass looked like a perfect fly, except for the tiny hole in its abdomen, but when I put the beam of pencil light behind it, it became translucent; somewhat like an air-filled miniature balloon!

Now I know why the Christmas cactus is also referred to as the Crab cactus!

22

Close Encounters with Ticks and Fleas

In the autumn of 1954, some six months after my arrival in Canada, I took up a homestead in northwestern Ontario in a region where there were no villages and few people and where the boreal forests dominated the environment.

Stepping into the black spruce sylva for the first time soon after sunrise during my second day in the region, I felt insignificant. I stood absolutely still, at first smelling my new environment, then slowly turning my head, looking and listening: to the calls of unknown birds, to the susurrus made by a gentle breeze as it stirred the crowns of the spruces, to the rustling of small, unknown creatures as they scampered through the understory. My first reaction to that vast green world was awe, but that emotion was soon banished by excitement.

"This," I said aloud to myself, "must be Paradise!"

It was, in a way, but I did not then realize that those who enter Paradise must be ready to be tested. First, after an interesting autumn, came the trial of winter. In early January the temperature plummeted to 40 degrees below zero, a cold that quickly froze exposed flesh and produced loud, rifle-like reports when moist tree branches were suddenly split by the frost's pressure. I soon learned to live with that cold, and I even enjoyed it at times, but I knew that my paradisical world would not forgive carelessness.

Then came spring. I forgot the dangers of winter as I listened to the calls of arriving birds, watched snowshoe hares romping in the forest, and paused often to gaze at azure skies across which scudded small white clouds. I spent one entire day in the wilderness, a day that began at early dawn and did not end until eight o'clock in the evening. Tired, hungry, and in need of a good wash, I entered my dilapidated home, coaxed life into the woodcoal cook stove and when the well water boiled, stripped and had a standing bath in a round galvanized tub.

Soon after I began to dry myself I became aware of an intense rectal itch. What was causing such discomfort? Naked and still damp, I ran for my shaving mirror and a flashlight — which was needed indoors at that time of the evening — and, contorting myself with great difficulty I became shocked when I saw a pea-sized, almost black creature affixed to one side of the outer rim of my rectum! The attack on a very private part of my body almost caused me to go into shock and I was about to grab the filthy thing and rip it away when common sense and my biological studies came to my rescue. I realized that I was the victim of a tick, although such awareness did not make me feel any better.

I knew about ticks in general, but the creatures I had studied in Europe had always belonged to those species that attacked domestic animals. It had never occurred to me that a tick would select me as its prey, much less that it would find such a private and tender part into which it would thrust its twin sucking tubes without my feeling its journeying under my clothing or, especially, when it was thrusting its sucking tubes into my flesh.

I abandoned further thought on how the tick got there, concentrating instead on a far more practical matter. How could I rid myself of the tick without running the risk of infection?

Remaining naked, I went to the small suitcase in which I kept my biology texts. Among these was one dealing with spiders and their kin, which included ticks and mites, for these creatures are related to the arachnids. Unfortunately, and although the text had a considerable amount of information, its authors had written not one word about the removal of ticks embedded in human anatomy. It seemed that I was on my own in that regard.

What to do? I knew that if I tried to pull out my unwanted host by brute force, it would almost certainly leave its twin suckers behind and, since I would have to grasp it by the inflated body, it would assuredly squirt into my flesh the contents of its sack, returning some of my partly digested blood and at the same time injecting into my system an undetermined amount of its own fluids, which would almost undoubtedly produce infection.

As I was on the point of dressing and heading for the nearest hospital, which was more than thirty miles way, I suddenly remembered that ticks do have an Achilles heel. Like the rest of us they must breathe! Naked as a jaybird, I went quickly to my well, which contained a partly immersed bucket in which I "refrigerated" my perishables. A minute later I dashed inside with a lump of butter sitting on the tip of my right index finger. I applied the butter, covering the beast. Then, squatting over the mirror, I watched and waited while wondering anxiously, "will it work?"

I had the presence of mind to time the event, so I was able to determine that the tick emerged ninety seconds later. My first thought was to squash the brute, but training held me back. I wanted to identify the creature and learn something about its habits, so I put the greasy animal in an empty can and, keeping an eye on it, returned to my textbook. I discovered that I was dealing with a wood tick, *Dermacentor spp.*

Soon afterward, I found a great number of the same kind, for the region was infested by the blood suckers during spring and early summer. There was not a time when I went into the forest that, on examining myself thoroughly the moment I got home, I did not find myself playing host to a few *Dermacentors*, albeit now that I was alert to them I quickly rid myself of all the unwanted passengers. Also, the ticks that I brought home were always fixed in accessible places and I developed a simple technique for their removal.

Examining that first tick of evil intent through my old microscope, I noted that its twin tubes were firmly affixed to its head. This led me to believe that if I thrust the tip of a needle between the tubes, above my skin, I should be able to push them out without any problems. To test this theory, I went into the forest and invited one or more ticks to help themselves. In fact, arriving home I found that the invitees had brought their friends: I had acquired seven ticks. But the needle trick worked and the first invited batch of lodgers were ejected in two minutes flat. From then on, I did not worry about ticks. Instead, I began to study them, but in as much as there are more than one thousand known species, I concentrated on *Dermacentor*.

Before ingesting blood, the male has a body of pale gray with brown spots on its legs. The female's body is a somewhat darker gray with tinges of yellow; her legs are brown.

Adults feed exclusively on the blood of mammals; so do the young, but these start on small animals, such as mice and voles. When full, they drop off and spend some time digesting and growing. When hungry again, they hang on the edges of shrubs and hitch a ride and a meal on somewhat larger mammals, such as foxes, groundhogs, and skunks that brush against their perches. When full, they drop off again, digest the blood, grow some more, and become adults, which usually feed on large animals, such as moose, deer, wolves, and, of course, humans.

While sucking the blood, a tick will also syphon into itself any bacteria carried by its host. Later, when a blood meal is digested, the bacteria remain alive inside the tick and when the creature finds another victim, the bacteria passes into the new host.

One species of tick (*Ixodes damini*) has more recently focused attention on itself as the carrier of a spiral-shaped bacterium (*Borrelia burgdorferi*) that is the cause of Lyme Disease.

Not all *Ixodes damini* carry *Borrelia* as passengers. But many do, and the bacteria are passed into the host while the tick is sucking blood. In their new quarters Borrelia thrive as they dine on the victim's proteins, breed, and then wait to be syphoned up by a new *Ixodes* so that their kind can in due time be spread to another host.

On a lighter note, Lyme Disease is curable. Now that the medical profession can identify the presence of the parasite by administering a blood test, and now that the symptoms are better recognized by doctors, the sickness, although unpleasant, is no longer life threatening in the majority of cases.

Fleas, like ticks, also bite people, as I'm sure everybody knows. In fact, fleas are probably the most notorious pests of humans and of other warm-blooded organisms. It is estimated that fleas were responsible for killing half the populations of Europe during two outbreaks of Bubonic Plague ("plague" is a term applied to any widespread disease among humans). The first major outbreak of the disease occurred in the four-teenth century; the second in the seventeenth century.

The fleas carrying the disease are believed to have been native to Egypt's Nile Valley. They were not, however, the primary hosts of the bacteria that caused the illness: the fleas sucked the blood of rats carrying the disease that is today known as *Pasteurella*. Although it is believed that many rats died from the infection, they nevertheless exhibited considerable resistance to the bacteria. But when these invisible creatures were syphoned up by fleas that later sucked the blood of a person, *Pasteurella* was introduced into the bloodstream of the human host. Then, if that person was later bitten by a flea that was not infected, the insect absorbed the bacteria with the blood that it sucked and so, during its next meal, was sure to infect another person. Thus, unknowingly, people passed on the disease to each other.

During the Middle Ages, the Plague, as it was generally known, infected and killed millions of people in Europe, Africa, and Asia. Although the bacterium is still alive and evidently well today, anti-bacterial medication controls the disease in the great majority of cases. Fleas, nevertheless, are widespread and continue to be pests of humans and other mammals.

Indeed, second only to humans — who have slaughtered more of their own kind than has any other living organism — fleas are almost certainly the most dangerous creatures on earth. Worldwide, some 16,000 different species of fleas that belong to the order *Siphonoptera* have been identified. In North America 250 species have been identified to date.

What can be done to rid a pet and its home of fleas? Animals such as dogs and cats are often responsible for unwittingly bringing fleas into the house, much to the alarm of the home owners. But it is useful to note that although they will happily suck the blood of cats and dogs and humans, fleas do not lay their eggs on their hosts, but rather deposit them in detritus such as fluff balls, minute bits of dry foods, such as cookie dust, and a wide variety of other tempting, but hardly visible foods that, no matter how clean a home may be, will always exist under rugs, in the tight spaces such as between seat cushions and chair bottoms, and in many otherwise inoffensive locations suitable for the development of flea larvae (which are called maggots).

Thus, although there are a number of effective insecticides that will kill cat and dog fleas when rubbed or sprayed on the bodies of household pets, such medications will not reach the flea maggots under the rugs or elsewhere. To kill the maggots spray-on medications are available. From personal experience, I have found that the majority are effective.

However, some pets, especially older cats and dogs, may inadvertently become flea breeders if they develop dandruff. In such a situation, a mother flea will lay her eggs within the pet's fur — maggot fleas love dandruff! It is useful to treat such pets with the necessary medication, which any veterinarian can prescribe.

Wolves and other mammals that give birth to their young in dens, where the floors consist solely of earth, do not pass on fleas to their young. If there should be any detritus on the earth floor, the urine of the young, with its high levels of ammonia, will kill any maggot that is deposited by a flea.

Over the years, and although I have had considerable experience with bears, wolves, coyotes, foxes, raccoons, and skunks, I have never found fleas on any one of these animals.

It may be (at a guess!) that the blood of wild carnivores is unattractive to fleas; on the other hand, it may be that because such mammals are great travelers they are much less likely to encounter concentrations of flea larvae. Since the animals move about, a sated flea may drop off its prey to lay her eggs in areas where the larvae are less likely to survive, for, although I am unaware of them, flea larvae are almost certain to be preyed on by creatures of one kind or another.

However those things may be, I cannot conclude this account of fleas without making reference to a story that was first told to me soon after my arrival in England from Spain, the country in which I grew up until my late teens.

At the time I was in London, visiting relatives. A cousin whom I had never before met sought to demonstrate his knowledge of natural history by telling me the story of how a fox rids itself of fleas, explaining very seriously that when a fox becomes infested (his word) by fleas, it scratches off a bundle of fur from its coat, picks the fur up with its mouth and, holding it as high as it can at the very tip of its muzzle, it heads for the nearest pond or river. Arriving at the shoreline, the fox enters the water and swims away, submerging all of its body except that part that stretches from the back of its head to its nose, the latter being held up so that the fur does not get wet.

The fox continues to swim and while it is doing so, it feels the fleas running up its soaking-wet body and one by one seeking refuge on the bundle of dry fur. Then, when the fox is quite sure that all the fleas it has been carrying have sought refuge on the fur, it lets go of the little bundle and watches as it and the fleas are swept away. It is then presumed that the fleas will eventually drown, or will die of starvation!

I managed to keep a relatively serious face as my cousin concluded his yarn, but in the end I had to laugh, believing that he was pulling my leg. But, no. He was serious! That was in August 1938. Between that time and 1939, when I was rescued from more crazy yarns by the war, I was told the same tale by a number of people, all of whom believed the fable. Is the story still being told, I wonder?

23

Acquaintance with Sharks

Films such as *Jaws* and lurid tales of shark attacks have given the world's selachians an undeserved evil reputation. This is not to say that sharks do not attack humans — they do. But compared to the vast numbers of people that flock to the sea every summer, the attacks are few and have been likened to the rarity of a person being struck by lightning.

I like sharks. I first began studying them when I was a child in Spain, catching small individuals and keeping them in tide pools every summer, until it was time for school again, when my captives were released. Years later, diving in various oceans, I came in contact with many sharks, some of which, being sixteen and seventeen feet long, could have easily killed and eaten me if human meat was as attractive to the breed as the scare literature would have us believe.

Observed swimming undisturbed in its own world, a shark is a beautiful creature. It is lithe and streamlined and quite without an equal. Wagging from side to side the last third of its body, displacing water with its large tail fin, a typical shark glides along at a cruising speed of about two miles an hour, its mouth held slightly open, teeth folded inward, out of sight, its staring eyes occasionally showing white rings, and its expression benign. Each lazy movement of the torpedo-shaped body causes the tight skin to wrinkle and to produce velvety coruscations that alter their colors in accordance with the light that slants into the upper layers of water.

Such things, viewed in conjunction with the undersea world, combine to create a silent fantasia that is more powerful and enthralling than the most captivating musical composition. A single shark traveling in this tranquil state while the tropical sun lances the ocean is a wonder to behold; a dozen or more similarly at peace offer an observer the ultimate in esthetic experience.

I formed these conclusions some fifty years ago while diving in the Red Sea, and although I have observed hundreds of sharks of different species during the intervening years, I have not changed my mind. I continue to hold sharks in high esteem, for I have gotten to know them better, to understand them a little more fully, and to admire them a lot. Above all, I respect them. Not just because even a small one is quite capable of killing me in the water, but also because sharks are creations that have adapted so wonderfully to their oceanic worlds that I consider them to be the most physically perfect of all the life forms to be found on land or in the sea.

Many observers claim that sharks are unpredictable and are therefore more dangerous than any other animal. They say that no shark appears to know what it is going to do next. However, such a sweeping generalization owes its origin to the fact that no one individual can claim to be a shark expert. At best, those of us who have studied these challenging and mysterious animals have learned to recognize different species by shape, size, color, and habitat. We can understand some of the traits exhibited in the members of a particular species, and we know a great deal about the anatomy of sharks, but we do not know the mind of a shark, and, therefore, we do not know how a selachian is going to react under any one of hundreds of given circumstances.

For me, such a lack of knowledge makes the study of these great fish truly fascinating, although in more recent times I have not had the opportunity to enter the shark's world. But if I do return to the Red Sea, I will do so in the knowledge that there are at least 350 species of sharks.

Soon after I became acquainted with sharks, when I was too young to form prejudices, I viewed them in the context of their environment, seeing them as inhabitants of a world that teemed with other life forms. And I accepted them as a part of the oceanic ecosystem while realizing that they could be dangerous. But then, I knew from a very early age that the sea itself was dangerous and that it contained many animals that could hurt me if they were molested or handled carelessly.

Some of these were capable of doing only minor damage, such as the sea urchins and jellyfish, but the pain they inflicted was severe enough to be avoided. Such encounters taught me to become cautious of all other life forms.

Soon after a somewhat painful encounter with a sea urchin, the Mediterranean Sea introduced me to my first shark. Later, drawing on my initial, rather callow awareness of it, the sea became my mentor. It taught me how to count before I was in the first grade because I simply had to know how many spines adorned a sea urchin's shell and how many tentacles were suspended from the body of a jellyfish. More important, the sea also taught me how to reason. It molded my adult life and it eventually turned me into a biologist.

When I took my trip in British Columbia's Inside Passage in the early 1970s, I had no particular goal in mind, or if I did, it was subconscious, perhaps an inner urge to recapture some of my childhood experiences in Spain. In any case, I set out from Victoria, British Columbia's capital, and headed north, not seeking to study anything more than the magnificent landscapes of mountains and beaches until I got away from the busier regions. Then I slowed down and, instead of tying up at marinas, as I had done thus far, I started anchoring in small, relatively hidden bays.

Eight days later, as I passed Vancouver Island's northern-most point of land and found myself looking at the endless sea, which came in restlessly all the way from Japan, I really began to enjoy the cruise.

Sitting at the helm, watching the gulls as they skimmed over the restless waves, I turned east and met the rollers head-on, feeling the power of the sea, the violent, up-and-down motion that has always thrilled me. I soon found myself semi-mesmerized, part of my mind still concerned with steering, and another part simply musing, noting the blue sky flirting with white puff-ball clouds, and the yellow-green of the advancing waves, and hearing again their boisterous sounds.

I felt at peace, entranced by my locale. Then, suddenly, I was startled by the sight of something that I instinctively felt could not be real. Yet there it was, perhaps four hundred yards away, a large creature moving northward. A thing that I knew could not exist, but that was yet moving against the waves; a creature that had four tall fins. Was I seeing a sea monster, I wondered? "No!" I spoke out loud as I set the throttle at full speed and aimed at the mysterious apparition.

Some five minutes later I had cut the distance by about half; as the boat began to approach the creature, if that was what it was, it seemed to increase its speed. Then, startling me at first, but immediately after causing me to laugh, the "creature" turned into two huge basking sharks. The great selachians had been moving in tandem, one about halfway ahead of the other as they cruised on the surface, their tail and dorsal fins appearing to belong to one, four-humped creature.

For a time I thought I would catch up with the baskers, but as I was about one hundred feet away and getting a fairly good look at them through binoculars, they both dove. I had the feeling each would probably have measured about thirty feet.

Basking sharks are docile plankton eaters, the largest of which is said to have measured forty feet. Those two were the only ones that I have ever seen. I was, of course, pleased to have had an opportunity to at least see them at a distance, but I did feel somewhat foolish for having mistaken them for a marine monster!

Before I came to Canada, I had returned to the study of sharks, at first within their own immediate environment, then afterward searching through the available scientific material dealing with the species. During that time, I dug into the distant past, researching such observers as Pliny the Elder, the Roman naturalist who referred to sharks as *pescecane* (dogfish), a name that is still used in Italy. Today, as I continue my land studies, I miss the oceanic world and its marvelous inhabitants. Perhaps I may yet return to the domain of sharks . . .

24
The Trickster

I was a newcomer to Canada and to the boreal forests of northern Ontario when I first became aware of the gray jay, a bird that has fascinated me ever since the moment of our first acquaintance. Not knowing the species, I was amazed when I stopped in a small clearing to eat a sandwich and was immediately approached by what I at first took to be somebody's pet songster.

The bird was fearless. It first perched on a branch about four feet over my head and only a couple of yards away. Then, as I removed the wrapping from the sandwich, it flew down and perched on my knee, emitting several low, musical whistles. When the bread was exposed, the bird craned forward and after I broke off a piece, it took it from my fingers before I had even offered it.

I was some seventy miles away from any human habitation, studying a population of snowshoe hares in a lake-land region north of Kenora, Ontario, so my initial assumption — that it was somebody's pet — struck me as being ridiculous. During the five weeks that I spent in the area, the jay invariably hopped on me every time I stopped for lunch, always eager to share my bread, peanuts, and even the hard beef jerky that was the filling of my sandwich.

Later, discussing my studies with a government biologist in Fort Frances, I mentioned the bird and asked about it. I first learned its species name, *Perisoreus canadensis*; then its common name, Canada jay (more recently the bird was renamed gray jay); finally, I learned its nicknames: camp robber and whiskeyjack.

Camp robber I could understand, although I did not consider my erstwhile friend a thief. Rather, it was my guest and companion! But whiskeyjack? Why, I asked, had it been given that name? My informant did not know. I was intrigued and asked other people about it, but no one seemed to know. A year later, when I was settled in my homestead in Ontario, near the Lake of the Woods, I asked myself: could the bird be fond of whiskey?

Since I happened to have a bottle of scotch and a bottle of rye in preparation for the approaching Christmas celebrations, and since, furthermore, I was now befriended by no fewer than nine jays, I decided to test them. First, thinking that rye might be the choice, I soaked some bread in the spirits and put it out. The jays flew to the offering at once, but after one brief sniff, they flew into a tree, scolding me with their harsh chattering call, one that they usually reserve for moments of crisis, or when disappointed.

I retrieved the rye bread and tried scotch whiskey. The birds repeated their previous actions and again scolded me and kept doing so until I gave them their usual offering of home-baked, whole-wheat bread.

Chagrined because it seemed that the origins of the name were lost forever, I accepted the "whiskeyjacks" without further question. Over the years, many different gray jays kept me company in a variety of wilderness habitats, and some even entered my dwelling to join me at the table. I grew more and more attached to the species.

One morning in 1971 when I was delving into Indian legends while taking a break from researching the waters of the Pacific Ocean and the coastlines of British Columbia's Inside Passage, I nosed my boat up to the floating wharf of the Kwakiutl village of Klemtu, on Swindle Island. Becoming friendly with the Native who refueled my boat, I learned about a being whom the Kwakiutls call Weegit, who is the spirit of mischief, a supernatural trickster who can become anything he wants to be. Weegit seemingly prefers to turn himself into a raven, but he can as easily become a leaf, a man, or even a killer whale. In any one of his many guises this mischievous sort of poltergeist rambles around teasing any-thing and everyone. If, coincidentally, some good comes of his tricks, well and fine, but that is not his principal intent.

Now, it will probably be hotly disputed by all astronomers when I state that it was Weegit, and not some cataclysmic explosion, that created the moon, but that is what I was told by the Kwakiutls. It happened thus:

When Weegit and the world were both young, the nights were pretty black. Weegit didn't like the dark, and he began to think of ways to get light after sundown, so that he could perform tricks on a twenty-four-hour basis. At first he could not think of any way to put a light in his night world, but after a time he remembered that the only source of light to be had after sunset was in the possession of a selfish and humorless old man who owned a globe called Na-gwa-chi. Now, he thought, if I can get hold of that globe, I can carry it at night and perform all kinds of tricks.

Weegit decided to turn himself into a little boy — a toddler who could quietly sneak into the old man's dwelling and steal the Na-gwa-chi. This he did. But the old man turned up before Weegit, who was carrying the globe, got out of the lodge.

The old man gave chase and, because the legs of a toddler are not capable of outdistancing the legs of even an old adult, Weegit was nearly caught. But, at the last minute, as the old man was reaching for him, Weegit threw the globe into the air and immediately afterward turned himself into a raven and flew away. To his delight, the globe stayed in the sky and slowly revolved around the earth.

I became intrigued by the story of Weegit and I determined to learn more about native mythology. Some months later, having read volumes of mostly irrelevant material written by early white explorers, I found a unifying pattern relating to a spiritual being whose various native names translated to "Trickster."

Weegit had trickster counterparts all over North America. And all of them were reputed to be able to instantly adopt any personality, or physical form that they chose, always doing so for the purpose of playing practical jokes upon humans. I concluded that the various pranksters were really one and the same spirit that was known by different names in different parts of the continent.

The trickster is "Weegit" on the west coast of Canada, "Old Man" among the plains people, "Coyote" further south, "Raven" in the Yukon, and, among the Algonkian people that occupy eastern Canada, he is variously known as "Glooscap," "Nanibush," and "Wisadkejack." Say this last name quickly in the Algonkian way and, to the English ear, Wisadkejack turns easily into whiskeyjack!

The Trickster chooses well when he impersonates the gray jay, a bird that approaches humans swiftly and silently, knows no fear, and speaks in many voices. Boisterously apparent at one moment, this jay can suddenly vanish and as quickly reappear where it is least expected. An opportunist at all times, Wisadkejack gets the jump on all other birds by nesting in February or early March, often when snow still lingers on the ground.

Gray jays conceal their nests so well that it is extremely difficult to locate them. Even if one tries to follow the flight of a bird as it is going to the nest, one is almost sure to be foiled, for the jay dodges and twists about, never going directly to the nest. If succeeding in finding a nest, however, one is confronted by a marvelous example of natural artistry, ingenuity, and architecture.

Ten to twenty feet above the ground, sometimes less, the nest is located deep within the shelter of evergreen boughs. It is woven with great care and amazingly accurate proportions from a wide variety of materials that are sorted for their insulating values and layered according to texture. The material is woven in such a manner that when the hen sits on the nest, its rim fits her body so perfectly that the eggs are sealed off from the outside world and very little of the mother's heat escapes from the nest. This allows incubation to take place at a time when temperatures can drop to well below the freezing mark.

The innermost lining of the nest, on which the chicks will incubate, is composed of the finest substances, such as feathers, shredded caterpillar cocoons, spider silk, animal fur, and moss. The next layer consists of slightly coarser materials, such as grasses, old leaves, pieces of lichen, evergreen needles, and bits of bark. Lastly, the outermost layer is constructed from coarse twigs and birch bark, its materials protecting the more delicate inner layers and at the same time serving to anchor the nest securely to the tree branches.

While the hen sits, her partner is busy finding insects and ferrying them to her. He may also feed her frozen, but palatable, berries from the maple leaf viburnum (*Viburnum acerifolium*), as well as food that is scrounged from humans if any live in the vicinity of the whiskeyjack's territory.

The female lays from two to six eggs (usually three or four) that are pale green and blotched and spotted at the big end with olive or pale gray. She incubates on her own, and the young emerge from the eggs between sixteen and eighteen days later. When, at about the age of two weeks, the chicks leave the nest, they resemble their parents not at all, being sooty gray and sporting a black head.

Taking all such things into account, it did not surprise me that the Trickster chose the gray jay as one of his alter egos!

25
An Angry Bittern

Gronk, as I was to name him, was found on a grassy verge outside a high school in Haliburton Village, Ontario, in the early autumn of 1988. He was taken by an unidentified man to veterinarian Dr. Laurie Brown, who noted a severely fractured (displaced) left femur. The break was located at mid-thigh and the lower part of the limb was hanging by a section of skin.

Dr. Brown skillfully applied a splint that she fashioned out of a plastic syringe container split down one side so that it could be easily clamped around the leg from hip to ankle. The tube was then taped and the tape extended to partially bind the foot so as to prevent Gronk from putting his full weight on the limb. She then telephoned me, knowing that I had some experience with the rehabilitation of birds and mammals.

I accepted the care of the bittern, but soon found that it was a finicky eater who rejected all the foods that I offered, including a dead mouse, strips of chicken, strips of beef, and strips of trout with skin attached. Feeding the bird became a problem.

I decided to force him to eat, but I soon found that such treatment was easier said than done. It was also dangerous — every time I opened his cage and reached for him, Gronk lunged for my hand with his quite formidable beak while emitting the hoarse call that had originally caused me to name him. Nevertheless, I did force-feed him for the first four days, fearing that he would otherwise die of starvation. Then I managed to get a few live minnows from our own stream. This was not an easy thing to do, for at that season freshwater fish do not feed well. I soon found that our minnow population was down. There were no live fish to be had — or, at least, none that would willingly enter my minnow trap.

When I put the few unfortunate little fish that I had trapped into the bittern's water, he swallowed them in the twinkling of an eye, then hoarsely yelled for more. But more were not forthcoming, no matter how I tried to coax the fish into the baited minnow trap.

Two days later, after the bittern had regurgitated everything that I had laboriously and dangerously thrust down his gullet, my wife, Sharon, came to the rescue when she found a sporting goods store that had live minnows for sale.

Thereafter Gronk survived on a diet of the fish, eating an average of eight or nine daily (average size of minnow: three-and-a-half inches).

I realized that the bird would only accept food that had eyes, which should not have surprised me, for fish-eating birds swallow their prey head first so that the bones of the fish will pass through the digestive system without doing any damage. The eyes point the way down! But, I blush to confess, it took me some days to wake up to this fact of a fish-eater's life!

During the time that he was in our care, the bird remained healthy and continued to show a good appetite, but because it was impossible for Gronk to migrate in his present condition, and because of the problem of obtaining minnows for him in our rather isolated region, I contacted the Ontario Humane Society on October 24, to see if the bird could be transferred there and fed on a diet of store-bought smelts.

My request would most likely be approved, I was told, but I had to wait a few days for the decision.

Meanwhile, Gronk became very active and vocal if disturbed, although by then I had moved him from the original, small cage that had prevented him from being too boisterous and perhaps doing further damage to his leg. Now he was housed in a cage that was thirty-six inches long, twenty-four inches high, and thirty inches wide. The quarters were small enough to allow for ease of handling and to prevent harmful movements, but large enough to let the bird move about and feed; his food was placed in a water container twelve inches wide by six inches deep.

Just as I was about ready to take Gronk to Dr. Brown so that she could X-ray the fracture before his move to the Humane Society, we received good news. Through the efforts of the Ontario Society for the Prevention of Cruelty to Animals (OSPCA) and by courtesy of Air Canada, our bittern and another rescued by the OSPCA were to be flown free of charge to a bird sanctuary in Florida.

The following spring we received even better news. A Florida couple who read my books and write to me quite regularly went to visit Gronk in his Florida sanctuary. At first, the officials would not allow the couple to enter Gronk's cage for fear of contamination, but when they learned that the couple were fans of mine, the restriction was lifted. Later the couple sent us a photograph of him. He looked great! Later still, we learned that Gronk, fully recovered, was released.

26
The Star Washer

The scientific name for the raccoon is *Procyon lotor*, which in Latin means "star washer"; *Procyon* is the name of the first magnitude star, found within the Canis Minor constellation, and *lotor* means "washer." This name has been in use as far back as anyone can remember, when it was mistakenly believed that the masked, ring-tailed mammal washed all of its food — which it does not do.

How then, did the raccoon acquire a reputation that has been echoed again and again in the writings of naturalists for so many years?

The myth must have started with early European settlers,

who observed the animal wading in streams and at the edges of lakes and ponds hunting for food. Those early observers must have noted the raccoon's sensitive hands as they were constantly feeling for prey and catching frogs or minnows or clams.

When I first became acquainted with these intelligent animals, I accepted their supposed washing habits. But I wondered why they resorted to such behavior.

I searched the literature. One writer said that raccoons had poor salivary glands, or none at all, and for that reason they had to wet all their food in order to swallow it. I felt that such a lack in an animal was most unnatural and that the explanation seemed improbable. Another report said that raccoons have narrow throats and cannot properly swallow food. "Bosh!" I muttered as I stopped reading and instead junked the pseudo-scientific magazine.

Later I read that raccoons find pleasure from feeling the food under water with fingers that are extremely sensitive. This appeared to make some sense, yet I was not entirely satisfied by it. Nevertheless, I let the matter rest for some time, despite the fact that of the first fourteen raccoons that I studied, only one showed any interest in dunking his food. That one, significantly, had been a captive, raised as a pet by city people and kept in a cage until he became too much of a nuisance. They asked me if I could release him on my wilderness property.

At that time, I had a large feeding platform against the kitchen window of my house and all manner of wildlife would come to it in two shifts: the day animals, such as chipmunks and squirrels; and the night animals, including bears, flying squirrels, and raccoons, for whom I fixed a water dish at one end of the feeder. I used to sit beside that window and watch relays of raccoons eat the food that I put out, but, apart from drinking when they were thirsty, not a single wild raccoon "washed" its food.

After three years I was satisfied that I had solved the riddle. Hunting in shallow water, the raccoon often finds a pebble and feels it between its palms with a "washing" motion. When touch tells it that the item is inedible, the raccoon will drop it and keep searching. If it finds a clam, the raccoon will rub it just as it rubs a pebble, but the animal is able to tell by feel that the clam is edible. Fish and frogs wriggle, so they are immediately recognized as food and eaten without preamble.

I had feeding stations in various parts of my forest, none near water, and I continued to observe these. Many raccoons came to eat, but none sought to carry food to water.

During the last year of detailed observations, between May and late September, I studied fifty-nine raccoons while they hunted or ate in locations where there was no water. None had difficulty swallowing even the driest foods.

Then a second young raccoon was brought to me. He was only about three months old, loved to play-fight, and often got hold of one of my fingers. Whenever he did, I felt around inside his mouth. Always I withdrew a finger soaking with saliva.

Captivity, especially the kind that puts an animal in close confinement, changes the habits of wild creatures. Under such conditions, animals invent "games" out of boredom, but when housed in proper, stimulating enclosures, they display none of the wide variety of aberrant habits resorted to by improperly housed wild or domestic animals.

Captive raccoons are no exception and are unable to deny the inherent urge to seek their food with their hands, no matter how well catered to they may be. When they have had their fill of food provided by their keepers, they play at hunting by carrying surplus food to the water and losing it, then recapturing it.

Raccoons range over most of South America, Mexico, the United States, and southern Canada and are related to bears. Like their big "cousins" they eat anything and often.

Adult males may weigh more than twenty pounds (the record for one male in captivity was sixty-two pounds!); females weigh about 20 percent less.

In the southern United States, raccoons are active year-round, but in the northern parts they put on large amounts of fat, develop a heavy, warm coat, and go to sleep in a hollow tree, a human attic, under a deadfall tree, in a cave, or in an abandoned groundhog burrow. While they sleep, they absorb their fat, emerging in spring a lot smaller than when they retired. But, despite sleeping through the winter, they are not hibernators, a term that applies to animals that become torpid when their temperature drops to one or two degrees above the ambient temperature. Such animals do not wake up — not even when handled — until spring, whereas raccoons will awaken if disturbed and, in any event, will begin to prowl through the forests in January, which is the start of the breeding season in the northern parts of their range.

27

Eastern Cougars: Fact or Fiction?

On a bitterly cold, but sunny, morning in mid-December, 1954, an eastern cougar crossed Highway 11 at a point some forty miles west of Hearst, Ontario.

The cat was traveling south, and had leapt across the snow-filled roadside ditch to land belly-deep on the other side at a location slightly more than one mile west of the Nagagami River.

As a recent immigrant, I did not think it strange that I should find signs of cougar in that isolated region. These felines, I knew, were native to Canada. So, apart from being excited by the sightings, I assumed that I had made a routine discovery.

I had left Toronto four days earlier to take up a homestead south of the Lake of the Woods, unaware that Highway 11, then the only trans-Canada land route, was almost deserted west of Hearst and continued to be so for 135 miles, until it reached Longlac.

The temperature was 40 degrees (Fahrenheit) below zero, but the sky was clear and the sun brilliant, circumstances that prompted me to stop the car, drink some hot coffee, and spend a short time exploring the first boreal forest I had ever seen. Finding the cougar tracks was an unexpected bonus.

Historically, the cougar has one of the most extensive ranges of any mammal in the western hemisphere. It was at one time distributed from east to west right across North and South America and from Patagonia, on the southernmost tip of South America, to northern British Columbia and, more rarely, to the southern part of the Yukon Territory.

My training in biology prompted me to measure the clear imprints left in the crisp snow just off the asphalt. The tracks of the front paws measured three-and-three-quarter inches long by four-and-a-half inches wide. The spoor left by the back feet measured three-and-one-quarter inches long by three-and-three-quarters inches wide.

Experience gained in Africa allowed me to determine that the roadside tracks had been left by a walking animal whose stride (the distance between front and rear paw prints) varied between fourteen inches and sixteen inches. After recording these measurements, I looked across the ditch and saw the marks of the cougar's landing.

Wading hip-deep in snow, I examined the clear imprint

of the cat's body. By measurement, the distance from chest to haunches was fifty inches. The paw marks were too deep to note. A long gash in the snow behind the imprint of the haunches, however, had clearly been made by the animal's long tail. This drag mark was fourteen inches long and was deeper in the middle than at its ends, suggesting that the tail had been upcurved on landing.

I followed the trail into the forest. After about 1,200 yards the holes made by the paws as the cougar bounded through the deep snow gave way to clear imprints left on the surface of a well-traveled game trail. About 1,500 feet later I found a scratch mound (a typical feline territorial marking made when scratching up dirt and twigs to cover fecal deposits). Uncovering the mound, I examined three scats, the longest measuring five inches, with a diameter of one-and-a-half inches. Moose hair and bone chips were readily noted.

Because I was not equipped for wading in snow while wearing ankle boots, I returned to my car and continued my journey.

One month later, in Fort Frances, I went to the Ministry of Natural Resources office and reported my findings to the resident biologist. He scoffed at my report, noting that the eastern cougar had been extinct in Ontario since before the turn of the century and telling me that the tracks I had seen had probably been made by a bobcat.

I left the office knowing that the signs I had examined and measured had been left by a cougar.

Seven years later, on the sandy shoreline of White Lake, northwest of White River, I found more cougar tracks and three territorial scratch mounds, all of which I opened and examined. The next evening, returning from a canoe trip along a stream that feeds the lake, I saw a cougar from a distance of perhaps three hundred yards. The animal had been drinking when my canoe rounded a bend. I expected it to dash back into the forest immediately. Instead, water dripping from its muzzle, it stared at me for a few seconds then strolled away.

In 1969 I saw my second — and last, to date — eastern cougar, this time briefly. The sighting was about one thousand yards north of a small lake that feeds the Mattawa River. Our encounter was brief but unmistakable, for it occurred in July, in brilliant sunshine, while I was resting on a rock outcrop.

The cat strolled out of the bush, saw me immediately, and ran at full speed into the trees.

Those sightings and signs convinced me that the eastern cougar, although scarce, continues to survive in Ontario. Later, after completing a nine-month study of cougars in British Columbia, I wrote a book about my experiences with one particular male cat. The book was published in 1983.

A short time after publication, I was telephoned by a woman who, with her husband and family, operated a tree farm near King City, Ontario, a half hour's drive north of the city of Toronto. She said that all members of the family had seen a cougar on their property and that it had gone close to their home. The sightings had been reported to the Maple office of the Ministry of Natural Resources and biologist Tim Rance went to investigate.

Discussing the sightings with him recently, he told me that tracks lifted from the scene were made by a large canid, and not by a cougar.

"But from talking to all those involved, I left the location convinced that they had, indeed, seen a cougar," he told me. Rance added that it was likely that the animal was just passing through the area while seeking a more suitable range than the valley of the Humber River.

One year later, soon after my wife, Sharon, and I moved to the Norland area, the Ontario Provincial Police issued a public warning concerning a cougar that had been sighted in the surrounding region.

A local trapper next told me that he had actually seen the animal, while friends of ours, who live in the village of Uphill, were awakened late one night by what they described as "unearthly screams." Questioning three members of the family, their descriptions of the sounds tallied with the breeding season cries uttered by a female cougar.

Between 1983 and today, a number of my readers in eastern Canada and northeastern United States have written or telephoned me to describe sightings of cougar, or to report tracks and territorial scat mounds.

I believe that the eastern cougar still exists in small numbers. I also believe that it should be placed on the endangered species list and rigorously protected.

28
To Kill or Not to Kill

As a species, at least during recorded history, humans have had great difficulty drawing a line between killing in order to sustain life and slaughtering for sport, or for territorial or ideological ambitions. If our species cannot learn to draw such a line, we will, in the not too distant future, destroy our environment. Such a cataclysm, of course, would also destroy the human race.

The words "kill" and "slaughter" apply equally to all forms of planetary life. Thus, when a tree is felled, it is killed. When a forest has been cut down, it is slaughtered — and its death causes the death of the many other living things that depend on it. In such ways an entire ecosystem is destroyed, albeit the damage may not be immediately apparent.

However, although humans may be confused about killing for need or greed, we readily distinguish those organisms that we deem to be useful to us and those that are believed to be not useful, or outright bad.

I am often asked, when talking about a bird, or a mammal, or a plant: "What is it good for?" I usually answer by asking the questioner: "What are you good for?" Often he or she will bristle and retort: "Well, I'm a human being!"

I believe that the time has come for us to see the environment and its life forms as a unity. At present, too many humans continue to show concern only for the "good" animals — those that offer "sport" when hunted, or money when trapped — while they ignore the many others that have no "usefulness," those that are considered to be pests.

For instance, killing bears has become big business in North America. The financial value of a black bear is such that legal hunters, as well as poachers, are out there killing as many as they can get in their sights, be they males, females, or cubs.

Conservatively, a black bear is worth about $1,000 (Cdn.) to a licensed hunter, or to a poacher. Why? Because of the value of the bear's organs!

A bear's gall bladder will net a bear killer $200 (Cdn.). It will later sell in Korea or other Asian countries for at least $5,000, being prized in the East for its supposed medicinal values. In Canada and the United States, bear claws net the animal's killer between $4 and $8, depending on their size. The bear's two canine teeth will net a hunter at least $7 each, and the bear's paws, eaten as a delicacy in parts of Asia, are worth $20 each here and up to $150 in Korea. Next, the killer can sell the hide for at least $150, and the head, especially that of a large male, mounted and gussied up, will retail in the United States or Canada for a minimum of $500. That leaves the bear's meat (his or her very essence!), which is either consumed by the hunter or sold to armchair "sportsmen."

Another good source of income is trapping. A number of people in my community recently tried, to no avail, to help a female fox whose leg was held fast by a leghold trap. The animal was clearly in great pain as she dragged the trap and its long chain through the shrubbery. But despite the fact that several people appealed to the district office of the Ontario Ministry of Natural Resources, no help was forthcoming. In fact, one caller was told by an official: "Don't worry. It will chew off its leg."

As it happened, the fox, which had a litter of kits, was later seen limping along, evidently having managed to rid itself of the trap. Presumably, she was also able to take care of her young, although being partially incapacitated by her injury, her ability would be impaired.

Nature cannot be measured in economic terms. We cannot continue to think of "natural resources" that have been expressly placed on earth for humans to "harvest" at the expense of the whole environment.

We must take responsibility for our own survival and must therefore learn at an early age how to live effectively within our own habitat. Parental teaching begins this process, but no animal — nor, indeed, any living thing — can hope to survive unless it constantly seeks to take account of the influences that surround it after it has left the den, the nest, the nursery, or when the seed has fallen from the plant.

Humans have lost some of their basic animal instincts. Civilization, although it has offered us some great advantages, has also given us some serious disadvantages. And perhaps the most dangerous disadvantage — in terms of survival within our natural world — is that today's public too readily allows science, politics, and industries to run the affairs of the world from within the cloisters of academies, the cabinets of political power, the boardrooms of big business, and the meeting halls of unions.

Some of these scientific, political, and/or industrial developments may well be beneficial, but those that are not, which are probably the majority, remain outside of the awareness of most people, at least until they become already entrenched in society. If it happens that a particular technological development, political decision, or scientific "breakthrough" turns out to be harmful (and many have done so), the public may learn about it only when the damage has already become irreversible.

Thus, while an animal remains in constant touch with its world and especially with matters that pertain to its home range (and therefore to itself and its group), humans are not so informed and, indeed, have surrendered their power to an elite minority.

This is not to say that scientists, politicians, teachers, industrialists, and union leaders are deliberately working against the public good, although this, too, has occurred in the past, or that they are abusing the privileges of their positions. The majority are probably dedicated men and women who are conscientiously doing their jobs to the best of their abilities.

Deliberately or otherwise, technocrats, whether they are academics, industrialists, teachers, or public relations dispensers, obscure the meaning of their published work by tailor-making terms to fit their particular specialties or products. And many professionals have become so caught up with jargon that their papers, lectures, or promotional materials are all but unintelligible. For example: Why would one want to refer to a biological community as a biocenosis?

Jargon has increased radically during the last half of this century and has reached the point today where relatively few laypeople are given an opportunity to understand scientific and technical papers. For this reason, the public and the media are often unaware of the disparities that exist between the natural world and the synthetic, pollution-dominated environment that science, industrial technology, and political expediency have created. Many individuals are now baffled. They feel helpless and wonder uneasily about the continued survival of the world while asking: What can I do?

There is much that the individual can do. Once we understand the workings of nature, we readily see that the environment is a fragile place; and we can then judge intelligently the positive or negative effects of those scientific, technological, and political developments that surround us — and, also, the results of our own behavior. An informed and responsible citizenry is the watchdog of monolithic systems. It is no accident that whenever a dictator has risen to power the intellectuals in society have been persecuted.

Those who have children in the school systems, or even at university level, can seek to change the macabre focus of the "death studies" that are presently taught in high schools. Instead of learning how to dissect dead matter, students should be guided by the vibrant and rewarding "curriculum of life." Individually, we can convince the school boards that biology should not begin with the study of cells and the dissection of animals. We can talk to teachers and persuade them to study the whole animal, how it lives, how it behaves, how it interacts with the natural world: this is "skin out" biology — as opposed to "skin in" biology, which concerns itself with death so that the organs and cells of animals can be more readily studied.

It is not necessary to be a biologist to appreciate the beauty and peace of the undisturbed natural world, or to feel the joy of watching animal life in action. If we begin to understand the influences that govern all life forms — the sun and the moon, the atmosphere, the oceans and tides, the rivers and lakes, the rains and snows, the forests and the soil, the planets that surround us, and, finally, our neighbors the animals and the plants — we are already more than halfway toward our goal: the tranquility and pleasure that result from such an acquaintance with nature will urge us to share it with others, especially with our children. It will also make us want to conserve the environment so that it may last for all time.

29
Spirit of the Wilderness

I stand alone within the cloistered forest and I listen to the voices of the birds as I tape my thoughts and experiences. The birds are leaving, heading south. Many species have already gone, but sporadic flights wing over my head as I now walk quietly toward the nest that the red-tailed hawks built in the spring — a bulky, cup-shaped structure of twigs and small branches that sits in the crown of a large aspen.

I had noted the nest some time after the eggs had hatched and I had watched the growth of the eyases on a regular basis. I was present when they launched themselves into space for the first time. Two of the young went first. They left a noisy sibling tottering on the edge of the nest.

The more daring eyases flew well, beating their wings strongly, but yet not quite able to avoid small branches. Each time they hit a twig, they reeled and dropped a few feet; but they always recovered and, six minutes (by my timing) after they left the nest, they joined their parents.

The loner, its frantic calls being ignored by the adults, spent forty-seven minutes plucking up its courage, then it managed to launch itself and, surprising me, flew strongly, rising between the trees without colliding with branches and soon joined its siblings and parents. I wonder: Did the fact that it was flapping for forty-seven minutes help it to fly by exercising the wing muscles?

Now, the sun is already on its way down, highlighting the tops of the trees with incandescent orange and yellow hues that slant skyward. As I watch the colours, I hear the geese honk. The gaggle is behind me, but moving in my direction. I turn, looking up, and moments later a large flock of Canadas arrow above me, dark silhouettes moving swiftly below the colored sky, every member honking farewell. Soon they are gone, out of sight and out of hearing. And suddenly, or so it seems, dusk is trading places with the sun.

I look at the ground, at the curled, dead leaves that carpet the boreal floor. And then I look up, at the naked crowns of the poplars and at the larches, which shed all their needles about one week ago. Their condition advertises the imminent arrival of winter. This, then, I believe, is the last day of autumn. It is the time that I always think of as the paean to the fall season, when, with a final blast of riotous color, the wilderness makes ready for winter. But we, that is to say, the wilderness and I, have to wait for Boreas to finish inhaling before he can release his frost-laden breath upon the land and on all the living things that dwell on it, above it, and under its surface.

I realize that the forest has changed its personality. I stand quietly. I don't have to wait very long before the sun sinks lower and the dusk becomes more somber. Now, the sylva and I give welcome to the edge of night, and for the time that will soon offer newness. High above me, another flock of geese is winging south. They are invisible, flying high, but their voices, although faint, reach me. I remain still, listening until the honking cries fade away.

I was about to put away my notebook, but I decide to continue writing. I am now sitting on the trunk of a downed larch, an old giant whose death has been accelerated by bark beetles. It is 4 p.m. I have spent nine minutes listening to the howls of a pack of wolves. They are quiet now. They must have been about a quarter of mile away from me. The wolf's voice always thrills me, despite the fact that I have listened to it many, many times.

I well remember the first time that I heard a wolf singsong. It was during the autumn of 1955 and it had sounded mournful to my ears. How would I feel, I wondered, if I could find the calling wolves and see them launch their song? Not long afterward, I was able to answer my question.

I was in muskeg country of Canada's northland and it was late afternoon. As I am doing now, I sat on a downed tree in a reflective mood, feeling at peace with the world and with myself. That was when the wolves howled. Their voices were loud. They were near. I rose and moved toward the calls, the green muskeg mosses carpeting my steps and I circled in order to put myself downwind of the pack. Then, guided by the intermittent calls, and moving slowly, I walked toward the howlers.

Soon afterward, I saw the leader. As I had surmised — for no valid reason, however — he was large. He sat on his haunches on a bare granite rock, a monolith that stood alone in an area of trees and relatively flat land. The upper part of the wolf's perch was relatively flat, but my field glasses revealed that it was dressed by mosses, lichens, and, lower down, by clinging liverworts. I could not see the rest of the pack.

The wolf appeared fully relaxed, his bushy tail lying in a graceful curl by his side, hips spread, his front legs close together, feet set squarely between his extended back paws. When I first saw him, the position of his back traveled straight toward his head, which he held at an angle so that his muzzle pointed downward.

Searching his surroundings with the glasses, I failed to see the members of his pack. From my vantage, he sat silhouetted against the green spruces and, as I was watching, he brought his broad head slowly up; and he raised his muzzle until it pointed directly at the obscuring skies. His mouth opened wide, so much so that I could see his gleaming fangs, and the red of his tongue, and the paler carmine of his gums.

Then he howled. Long, tremulous, loud . . . it was a haunting melody that was immediately joined by the invisible pack. I felt a chill enter my body and the hair on the nape of my neck prickled as it rose, and I was unable to move. It wasn't fear that held me in a trance. I know fear; I have felt it too many times to fail to recognize it. This was a new feeling, a new sensation and excitement that came to visit me in the presence and sound of that wolf. I remained immobile as the pack continued calling, launching their songs, pausing, and singing again. Then, at last, the leader responded to the pack. His flattened ears became erect and he howled more, a short call that was again answered by a chorus. The wolf jumped off the rock, paused momentarily to stare fixedly in my direction, then trotted away. He was, I became sure, going to become reunited with his pack. I was equally sure that he had known of my presence from the moment that I began to circle.

Released from my trance, I set out for home, but ever since that afternoon there has been new meaning for me in the howl of the timber wolf. Now, as I listen to the wolves howling, I feel that it is the spirit of the wilderness that is calling to me.

Appendix:
The Care and Rehabilitation
of Animals

The care, housing, and rehabilitation of wild mammals and birds are responsibilities that should not be undertaken lightly by the inexperienced. Neither should wild animals be "adopted" by those who do not have the proper housing facilities for their wards, or who are not able to devote sufficient time to a task that requires considerable patience and awareness of the rescued animal's needs.

Before addressing the subject of wild animal care and rehabilitation, however, it is first necessary to define what is meant by the word "animal," a term erroneously believed by many to apply only to mammals. The word derives from Latin *anima*, which means "breath," and post Christian era, was most often taken to mean the human soul. Animal describes all organisms that are not a plant or a fungus. Thus, when discussing rehabilitation in general terms, the use of the word applies equally to mammals, birds, fish, reptiles, amphibians, and insects.

Does the Animal Need Rescuing?

The first thing that a would-be rescuer must ask is: Does the animal need rescuing? This query applies particularly to fledgling birds, which, at the stage when they are just about ready to fly, often flutter out of the nest. Made tearful by the experience, they often perch on bushes or sit on the grass cheeping loudly for their parents. Too frequently, well-meaning people pick up such fledglings and "rescue" them. If the fledglings are left alone and watched for a time, would-be rescuers will see that the parent birds feed the fledglings and, by example, teach them to fly on their own.

Similarly, some young mammals that have strayed from the mother may call in distress, either because they think they are lost, or because they have become afraid. Usually, the mother will either return for the lost one, or the young will use its keen faculties — hearing, scent, vision — to find its own way back to the den or to its wandering family. Here again, quiet observation from a proper distance (which depends on the species and the age of the wildling) will in time reveal whether the animal is really lost, or just temporarily separated from its parent(s). Incidentally, such quiet observation is a good way to learn about wildlife.

Assuming that an animal is truly orphaned and is too young to fend for itself, it should first be examined visually:

- Is the orphan injured?
- Is it able to walk or fly short distances?
- Does it look ill?
- Is it behaving in what may be termed an unnatural way?

For beginners these questions can be hard to answer. However, there are many books available that deal with animal behavior, such as: *The Mammals of Canada*, by A. W. F. Banfield; *The Birds of Canada*, by W. Earl Godfrey; and *Introduction to Canadian Amphibians and Reptiles*, by Francis R. Cook. All are published by the National Museum of Natural Sciences and should be available in most libraries, or can be purchased through a book store. Also, the American National Geographic Society publishes such excellent books as *Wild Animals of North America* and *Water, Prey and Game Birds*. Note that none of these books discusses diseases of animals or animal rehabilitation, but they will give their readers an understanding of the biology and general behavior of mammals, birds, amphibians, and reptiles.

A word of caution. Many people believe a young wild animal will make a nice pet, especially when an orphan is the cuddly furry kind, such as a raccoon. But wild creatures do not become easily domesticated. When adult, the majority make very bad pets! Nevertheless, one should realize all animals, regardless of species — just like humans — are individuals. *Some* may take to domestication, but, again, the great majority will not become pets. In my experience, and with some rare exceptions, those people who have tried domesticate wild animals usually fail, sometimes when they find they cannot "house train" an orphan, and often when the animal bites its keeper. Thus, I emphasize: Wild animals belong in their proper habitats!

Mammals

Unless an orphaned mammal is very young, it will usually put up a bold front when approached by a human rescuer. It may have very small teeth and it may weigh only a few grams, but it will probably snarl, mouth agape when approached.

This is usually a bluff. The animal is fearful; it seeks to intimidate its would-be rescuer, believing that it is faced with an enemy. If you pick the animal up quickly — but gently — by the body (behind the head), raise it to chest level, and then cuddle it against the left side of your body, over the heart, most young orphans will quickly settle down. The human heart, although it beats more loudly than that of small mammals, has an almost immediate calming effect on fearful young animals.

If an orphan has already acquired a full set of its first teeth, it would be wise to wear leather gloves. The orphan may be healthy, but a bite — even a small scratch — can sometimes lead to infection.

Housing

Once an orphan has been rescued, it must be suitably housed. Depending on its age and size, a sturdy nesting box suitably fitted with bedding should be provided. Very young mammals that require bottle-feeding should at first be housed in relatively dark quarters that are spacious enough to allow modest wandering, but not so large that the animal will stray and become disoriented.

If the youngster is not fully furred, it should be kept warm. Use a hot-water bottle, an electric heating pad — on low heat and placed underneath the housing and not under the animal itself — or a heat lamp. Very young mammals have poor heating systems, and cold can induce hypothermia (when a young animal becomes too cold), which may quickly kill an orphan. The temperature for coyotes and foxes, for example, should vary between 82 and 85 degrees Fahrenheit for the first seven or eight days of life. After that, the correct temperature should be between 70 and 75 degrees Fahrenheit until the animal is well furred, strong, and healthy, when its own heating system maintains correct body temperature. In an emergency, the best way to heat an animal up is to place it against your body, under the clothing. This may cause a tickling sensation, or scratches, or staining (and odor) by bowel and bladder discharges. That is the price to pay — it goes with the territory!

When the orphan becomes active, that is, when fully furred and starting to need solids as well as formula, it should be allowed to exercise. Depending on the species, it should have a fenced area in which to wander and a number of "toys" with which to develop its coordination and muscles.

Raccoons, for instance, do well in a cage eight or ten feet long, four feet wide, and six feet high. The cage should be equipped with a climbing apparatus, odds and ends such as rubber bones and toys, and short logs with holes drilled into them that are large enough for a raccoon's hands to enter. A nesting box of proper size should be a part of the cage, preferably outside it, with an entrance leading directly into the exercise area.

Note: Wild mammals should never be constantly confined in small quarters. The cage should not be considered a permanent home, but as a temporary holding place for those times when you are out of the house and at night, when the household is asleep in bed. Take the orphan out of the cage at intervals and allow it to roam (under supervision) in the house and/or take it for walks out of doors. After close acquaintance, most young mammals will follow the rescuer much as they would follow their own mothers.

Ideally, a well-fenced enclosure should be provided outside your house. Use two-by-four inch strong mesh, such as corn-crib wire (not chicken wire, which is too weak). To prevent the orphan(s) from digging out, bury the wire at least one foot in the ground, or lay two feet outward from the upright fence and bury about one foot at a downsloping angle, so that the part nearest the fence is shallow (about five inches deep) and the end of the wire is dug in at the one-foot level (this creates a slope). Most mammals that are likely to try to dig their way out begin to do so at the fence itself, thus immediately encountering the buried wire. After a few digs at different locations along the fence line, they usually give up. If climbing animals are to be contained, the enclosure should be roofed by wire mesh.

Diet

Very young mammals feed often and sleep a great deal. When their belly is full, they usually curl up and go to sleep almost immediately. If they do not, and show signs of distress, something is wrong: either they are still hungry, or they have eaten too much, or they are not well. If still hungry, some extra feeding will soon induce sleep; if too much food has been ingested, the resulting colic should end in due course, but some gentle massage of the bulging stomach will help.

Do not overfeed! How can you tell when a wildling has eaten enough, but appears to want more? Rule of thumb: Feel the stomach with one finger poking gently. If the tummy has the consistency of a soft-boiled egg, the animal will probably need some more feed; if it is the consistency of a hard-boiled egg, the animal has overeaten. The right "feel" should be that of a medium-boiled egg.

Young, nursing animals require formula feeding. Esbilac formula works well with members of the Canid family (wolves, coyotes, foxes) as well as with raccoons, bears, skunks, and most other young mammals. Cat milk (available at some pet stores and at veterinaries) can be used instead of goat's milk, or canned milk. Do not feed cow's milk. In an emergency you can use diluted cow's milk for a short time, or powdered skim milk.

It is best to add a small amount of pure glucose to the formulas of very young mammals. Wolf and coyote pups separated from their mothers before the first twelve days of their life are subject to cataracts that evidently occur because of glucose deficiency, which is supplied in the mother's early post-partum milk. Some pet animal milk substitutes may be glucose deficient, or they may have insufficient amounts for the animal's needs. Adding extra glucose to each is a precaution that will prevent blindness and, if not needed, will do no harm.

Feeding bottles and nipples will be required. Very small mammals are usually fed by eyedroppers. Pet stores today have an array of assorted bottles and nipples that will suit practically all young mammals. It is useful to have an assortment of such feeders at hand if you plan to become an animal foster parent.

When an orphan's gums begin to show signs of teeth (you can detect tiny, rough eruptions by *gently* passing a finger over gums), mix cereal food with the formula. For normal, healthy mammals, human baby food is excellent. For animals that have loose bowels, rice cereal will return them to normal if there are no intestinal problems, such as round worms (nematodes that are common in most wild animals). It is always a good idea to take stool samples to a veterinarian to have them tested for parasites.

After an animal is weaned, it should receive a balanced diet. Omnivorous animals, such as raccoons and bears, eat almost anything; nevertheless their diet should be as balanced as possible. Multiple vitamin tablets, crushed, can be mixed with such things as high protein dog food (kibble) and table leftovers, especially bits of fat. Or, for young animals, provide good quality puppy or kitten chow.

If animals are not to be released until autumn, you should

add sugars, such as molasses or even marshmallows, to their diet. Experience has taught me that animals usually select the food that they require in season. All of the more than 2,000 mammals that my wife and I have raised and rehabilitated during the past thirty years have expressed a need for sugars during the fall. You should also have on hand small salt blocks containing trace minerals for an animal to lick.

First Aid Supplies

Individuals who become involved with orphaned or needy animals should have a first aid kit in the house. This should contain the following items:

- antiseptic cream or lotion for cleaning and disinfecting minor injuries;
- boracic acid for bathing infected eyes;
- cotton batting;
- Q-Tips;
- wound powder (see a veterinarian for this);
- Pepto-Bismol or Kaopectate for diarrhea; and
- non-toxic flea powder, although most wild animals are exceptionally free of such parasites once they have been out of their dens for some time.

Also useful for weak or sick animals is a supply of "instant protein" such as Nutravit.

It is a good idea to take an orphan animal to a veterinarian as soon as possible after it has been rescued. A check-up may prevent disease for both the animal and its handler.

Handling Precautions

Bites and scratches from handling very young animals are rare, but when an orphan has reached the weaning stage, it has teeth that are usually very pointed and can inflict fairly deep bites. Such animals, already in a panic after being abandoned — in some cases live-trapped — will bite their rescuer if given an opportunity to do so. Wear stout leather gloves. Note that such feisty young creatures will quickly settle down when they realize that they are not being harmed and, on the contrary, are being fed and well housed.

Avoid fast, sudden movements when approaching or handling animals. Also avoid loud noise, such as blaring radios, thumps or bangs, or general chatter in the vicinity of a newly rescued orphan. I have learned that the human voice, uttered in quiet, well-modulated tones, has a soothing effect on frightened young animals. The words do not matter — nursery rhymes, poetry, even "baby-talk" will do. The important pacifier is the quiet, caring tone of voice.

When and Where to Release
These are not easy decisions to make! So much depends on the species of animal and on the territory that is being considered for release. It is not good to "load" the same region of wilderness with a large number of animals of the same species. Monitor the area ahead of the release. If, for instance, a survey reveals that the raccoon population in a region is high, no others should be liberated in that location. Then, too, all the care and expense of raising an orphan will be wasted if it is released too early, or if it is released in a territory incompatible with its needs in terms of its natural foods and, of course, an accessible supply of water.

Should a Wild Animal Be Immunized?
All mammals should be immunized for rabies, parvovirus, and distemper. This is a job for a veterinarian. To release unprotected mammals into a wild environment is an act of carelessness. The animal is likely to die of disease and,

more important, may help spread the disease. Protection is essential. Indeed, those who may become involved in handling wild animals on a regular basis should themselves receive pre-exposure vaccination. Consult your doctor on this topic.

All young orphans should be made accustomed to handling. Again, this does not mean that they should be turned into pets, but unless an adolescent animal can be safely and comfortably handled, its treatment (if it is injured or becomes ill) will be difficult, if not impossible.

Birds

As already noted, animals should not be rescued until they need rescuing. This applies especially to fledgling birds! However, assuming a fledgling does, indeed, need rescuing, it is important for the rescuer to understand that such fragile wards require a great deal of attention. Most fledglings, or naked neonates, need to be fed about every fifteen or twenty minutes on average, a task that can keep a human very busy!

The heating systems of newly hatched birds are inactive for some days after birth, so it is natural for them to feel cold to the human touch. If taken into an average-temperature house, all orphans will need is a comfortable nest made from material that will not entangle their clawed feet. Fledglings can be made comfortable on small branches, or in an abandoned bird nest placed within an appropriate cage.

Birds are early risers. The human household wherein one or more young birds live may expect to be awakened by first light unless the nest or cage is draped by a black cloth. This may be conducive to human rest, but can be harmful — even fatal — to the nestling(s), if the bird is deprived of food for too long.

Birds, especially swallows, are notorious for harboring lice.

Not to worry! Bird lice do not bite humans. In any event, for swallows, at least, lice serve as needed protein if parent birds are away too long from the nest. At such times, usually because of excessive heat and drought, when insects are scarce, parent swallows may hunt for up to forty minutes before they have gathered a sufficient number of insects for their brood. When this happens, the fledglings feed on their own lice, preening their newly emerging feathers and ingesting the lice that they trap in their beaks.

Bird Diet

Most young birds eat the insects brought to them by their parents. Almost any insect will do, but you will need to mash large "bugs." Catching insects for this purpose is time-consuming and difficult, so most bird rescuers rely on a variety of concoctions that are satisfactory, if not altogether perfect.

Most young birds will do well when fed a mixture of water-softened, high-protein dog food, chick feed, boiled egg, a little sand or loam, cereal food, and a pinch of powdered multiple vitamins. Bits of berries (strawberry, raspberry, blueberry) will be relished by ground nesters, while succulent caterpillars — somewhat mashed — and small insects will be welcome to insect eaters. Munched earthworms are also good, as are bits of raw liver. In effect, there seems to be as many bird diets as there are bird rescuers. Whatever works is good!

Because of the dedication, expertise, and hard work demanded by the job of bird rehabilitation, it is best left to those who already have experience and a good survival track record. The humane societies and other similar organizations know at least a few people who know how to raise young birds and are willing to do so.